THREE CATS,
TWO DOGS

THREE CATS, TWO DOGS

One Journey Through Multiple Pet Loss

DAVID CONGALTON

FOREWORD BY
WALLACE SIFE, PH.D

NEWSAGE PRESS
TROUTDALE, OREGON

THREE CATS, TWO DOGS
One Journey Through Multiple Pet Loss

Copyright © 2000 by David Congalton
ISBN 0-939165-37-6

NewSage Press
PO Box 607
Troutdale, OR 97060-0607
503-695-2211

web site: http://www.newsagepress.com
email: newsage@teleport.com

Cover Design by George Foster
Book Design by Patricia Keelin

The Cover is a montage of photos taken by David Congalton and Charlotte Alexander of their five animal companions: Topper and Triptych (center), Trio (bottom left), Tess (upper left) and Tripper (bottom right).

Printed in the United States on recycled paper with soy ink.

Distributed in the United States and Canada by Publishers Group West 800-788-3123

Library of Congress Cataloging-in-Publication Data

Congalton, David, 1953-
    Three cats, two dogs : one journey through multiple pet loss / David Congalton ; foreword by Wallace Sife.
        p. cm.
    Includes bibliographical references (p.).
    ISBN 0-939165-37-6 (pbk.)
    1. Pet owners—Psychology. 2. Cat owners—California—San Luis Obispo—Psychology. 3. Dog owners—California—San Luis Obispo—Psychology. 4. Pets—Death—Psychological aspects. 5. Bereavement—Psychological aspects. 6. Congalton, David, 1953- I. Title: 3 cats, 2 dogs. II Title.

SF411.47 .C66 2000
155.9'37—dc21
                                                        00-035123

For Charlotte, always
For Lynne Siegel, especially

"If there are no cats and dogs in Heaven, then when I die I want to go where they went."

– Anonymous

Contents

Acknowledgments

This journey from the dark side of my heart to the light of the printed page was anything but a solo effort. Far from it. Old friends and new acquaintances sprang up along every critical curve in the road, offering comfort, direction, and the courage to continue.

Psychologist Mary Speidell first encouraged me to let my emotions spill out on paper in the months immediately following the fire. For once I listened, and looking over the final result, I am ever so grateful for that initial nudge.

Susan Amerikaner, Conni Gordon, and Aleida Lund read early drafts of the manuscript and chased away any lingering doubt that this was a story worth telling. Had they not been so supportive so early in the process, I probably would have kept the pages to myself.

Elizabeth Lyon of Lyon's Literary Services in Eugene, Oregon gave the manuscript a more critical eye and calmly held my hand as I wandered wide-eyed into the labyrinth of the publishing world.

Fortunately I landed at NewSage Press. The ensuing editorial dialogue surrounding this book has been the most professionally satisfying of my twelve-plus years as a writer. Thank you to my publisher and editor, Maureen R. Michelson, for so deftly walking that fine publishing line between cautious critic and knowing cheerleader. Also, special thanks to NewSage Press designer Patricia Keelin for creating such a first class book, and to George Foster for his cover design.

I am honored to have Wallace Sife, one of the pioneers of the pet bereavement movement, provide the Foreword. His exemplary work as a psychologist, author, and founder of the Association for Pet Loss and Bereavement (APLB) has established Dr. Sife as a leader in the international pet loss movement. I value his insight and friendship in equal doses.

Greg McClure of Goodhelp in San Luis Obispo spent countless hours creating and maintaining my official web site at www.davidcongalton.com, which allows me to take my story to infinity and beyond in cyberspace.

Of course, none of this would have happened without the understanding of Charlotte Alexander. Charlotte has never hesitated to let me put our lives, our relationship, in the public eye. A writer who is married to such a person can have no greater support.

Finally, a personal nod to the late Jeff Fairbanks, the editor of the *San Luis Obispo County Telegram-Tribune*. A car accident in 1995 took him away far too early. Jeff was delighted to have me write about Topper in his newspaper, often featuring our adventures together on the front page. He always said I would write a book one day. Thanks, Jeff, for believing in me.

Foreword

This is a fine book, but just a few years ago it couldn't have been marketed. The subject of pet bereavement and bonding was still too radical, and no commercial publisher would have touched it. However, since the late 1980s the world has been waking up to this reality, and acknowledging the tremendous grief humans can feel over the death of an animal companion.

Although it is not designed as a textbook or self-help manual in pet bereavement, I see *Three Cats, Two Dogs* as an important contribution in this new genre of books. The reader is immediately swept up by the catastrophe, and David Congalton's articulate expression makes us feel we are his close friends, sharing this intimate loss and survival with him.

At the time of this writing it is estimated that there are over fifty-eight million dogs and sixty-three million cats in the United States. And these numbers are increasing, annually. A great majority of Americans now have or once had pets, and the average person is likely to have already experienced the death of at least one. Unfortunately, there still exist the last vestiges of a long-standing tradition of silence and judgment on the subject of pet loss and bereavement. Most pet lovers already know that a great many good people are very vulnerable to the deep personal grief and emotional stresses that result from this kind of tragedy. Even today, many who are bereaving for a dear pet still think they are alone with such feelings, and they are only now discovering the rest of us. The intense emotions arising from pet loss and bereavement used to be kept secret. It was too easy to become the victim of insensitive criticism and disapproval.

With the recent revolution in communications the concept of the global village has become more of a reality. Now, the public consciousness is rapidly becoming more aware that pets are everywhere around us. An hour's viewing of television will contain at least one ad or program that has an adorable pet in it. The Internet has exploded with web sites and countless pages dealing with every aspect of companion animals. And in 2000 it is anticipated that more than $22 billion will be spent on dogs and cats in the United States. We are living in a new age, where our pets are becoming more openly acknowledged as major loving influences on our lives. The times are changing, and with this we are discovering revisions in society's perceptions of companion animals.

David Congalton has stepped forth with a deeply moving account of life and death in his family of many beloved pets. Although most of us do not have multiple companion animals, this book offers us a new awareness and perception. Until now, it has always been too easy to pass off anyone with multiple pets as some sort of benign neighborhood eccentric. Indeed, there are still many pet lovers who do not appreciate what this is really like. This is a new kind of reading experience, sharing enormous love with us, and we are enriched by this contribution. These pages present a loving life and adventure with five unique companion animals. They were distinct members of the Congalton family and through the author's skill we are able to feel and begin to understand what this must have been like. When understanding is added to empathy we have a breakthrough in appreciation.

There are many new books coming out on the subject of pet loss and bereavement, but *Three Cats, Two Dogs* is different. The author's experience and poignant presentation is reminiscent of the fabled Phoenix rising from its own ashes. We discover how the tragedy expressed here is overwhelming, but endurable. And through this we also learn to recognize and learn so much about ourselves. The monumental message given is that we can survive such terrible loss without allowing ourselves to be destroyed. Paradoxically, the intense bonding and love experienced in this book actually becomes a subconscious natural life preserver in the aftermath of the tragedy. After finishing these pages, you will be left with a keener appreciation and love for all your pets, past, present, and future. And because of them, we all become better people as well.

– Wallace Sife, Ph.D.
  Founder and President, Association for Pet Loss and Bereavement (APLB)

Prologue

My wife Charlotte and I liked to tell our friends, "We always spell love with a T in our house." There were five special reasons why: Topper, Triptych, Tripper, Trio, and Tess. Three cats. Two dogs. One big happy family. Then we came home from a holiday party on December 14, 1997 to find the inside of our house engulfed in smoke and flames. All five pets were dead.

Just like that. Not one was spared.

Instead, every pet lover's worst nightmare, multiplied by five, suddenly, dramatically, unfolded before our eyes. And in the weeks and months to come, we would have to learn to face grief head-on and move forward.

More than three months after the fire, the crying bouts continued. I'm 44 years old, reasonably intelligent, and somewhat responsible. Yet, I have sobbed uncontrollably, almost daily. One minute I would seem fine; then suddenly, unexpectedly, I would start bawling like a baby. I cried more in the first three months after they died than in my entire life. Part of me felt shame, embarrassment, for not being able to stop the tear parade, for not being able to control myself. I wondered if it would ever go away.

The night of the Academy Awards in March 1998, I was supposed to meet Charlotte at an Oscar-watching party hosted by two of our closest friends. I dutifully showered and dressed to go out for the evening. I was looking forward to being with everyone, but I never got close to the front door. My mood suddenly shifted; I felt completely helpless.

Thinking of our beloved pets flared up ugly flashbacks to the fire—one painful memory leading to another, a complete emotional chain reaction. The teary meltdown began before Billy Crystal cracked his first joke. Overcome with grief, unable to move, I suddenly just wanted to be alone. More memories. More tears. There was no way I was going out to any party—friends or no friends. About ten minutes later, I managed to compose myself long enough to call Charlotte. She was in her car on the way to the party.

"I can't make it," I blurted through the tears. "I just can't."

"What's wrong, David?" my wife's voice crackled on the cell phone. "Is everything OK?"

Long pause as I struggled. "I can't leave tonight," I stammered. "I need to stay here."

Charlotte, who had battled through a few crying spells herself, understood immediately. We had been married for almost nine years, but never had been closer than during those first three months after the tragedy. We took turns being the strong one.

"I'm coming home," Charlotte announced. I didn't argue. After hanging up, I buried my face in my hands and slumped down in the hallway. Sitting there, crumpled up, I didn't understand what was happening. I wasn't sure anyone could.

There were certainly those who claimed to understand, those "I-know-exactly-how-you-feel" folks. They don't. Then there are those who should, but couldn't—or wouldn't. Some relatives never even bothered to bring the subject up during a visit barely two months after the pets died. My editor at the newspaper constantly urged me to find something else to write about. "Enough is enough, Dave," he argued. Even our close friends appeared to assume that everything was OK with Charlotte and me, that we had gotten on with our lives somehow.

No one really understood. But how could they? I wasn't even sure that I did. Three months after the fire and I still had enough tears to sink the *Titanic*.

So Charlotte rushed home and we huddled quietly in front of the television, blocking out the rest of the world, half-watching the awards ceremony, trying hard not to think of anything, or anyone. Later that night, when things had stabilized somewhat and my wife drifted off to sleep, I sat alone, again replaying the events of the past three months since the tragedy in my mind.

Enough, I finally decided. *I can't go on like this. No more nights like tonight.*

So I forced myself into our converted office and plopped down in front of the computer; the words seemed to write themselves. I cannot explain this sudden call, but it is a familiar ritual. I wrote a twice-weekly column for the local Knight Ridder newspaper in San Luis Obispo, California. During the last five years, I often turned this computer into a public confessional to share much of what was happening in my marriage and my personal life—our five animal companions were certainly an important centerpiece to both.

That night in March was another harsh reminder that my heart remains shattered in a million tiny pieces; that I am far from the happy and smiling man I so pretend to be publicly. I decided to put what was left of that heart on paper. At the time, I didn't know where my words would lead. Nor did I know if they would make any difference about the emptiness I felt. So I began. Words and thoughts about five very special animals. And sudden loss. And grief. And ignorance. And love, especially love.

As I wrote the story of my journey through this unbelievable loss, I quickly realized that this was also a celebration of having animals in our lives. There was never any hesitation for Charlotte or me to open our lives to animals. Topper, Triptych, Tripper, Trio, and Tess were always an important inspiration for my writing. Some of my favorite pet-oriented newspaper columns are sprinkled throughout the book, markers along the way to underscore the extent of our great joy, and profound loss.

I do this for me, and for Charlotte. But most of all, I do it to celebrate and remember them—Topper, Triptych, Tripper, Trio, and Tess. Three cats. Two dogs. Five reasons why the tears still refuse to go away.

ONE

No Home Is Complete Without A Pet

*C*harlotte and I are card-carrying animal lovers. It's the bond that unites us. We are the kind of people who consider our animal companions to be members of the family, plop-on-the-couch, stretch-out-on-the-bed members of the family. We're the ones, like those reported in a highly publicized Gallup Poll, who typically give our animals Christmas and birthday presents and have proud photos of them scattered throughout the house. We're among the millions of pet lovers whose combined spending is presently about $21 billion on our animals every year.

Some people consider their pets to actually be their children. Anyone who has ever visited our home and seen the photos of our gang plastered around the house—along with the basset hound night light, the cat salt-and-pepper shakers and the black cat clock in the kitchen—certainly knows how much we love animals. Animals are definitely part of the family.

Yet, we've never been comfortable with the idea that pets are our children. Topper, Triptych, Tripper, Trio, and Tess were our companions, deserving of our love and devotion, yes. However, we tried to remain reasonably grounded about our relationship with them. For example, when I was growing up in suburban Chicago, my parents liked to have the family dog, a spunky labrador named Blackie, join us at the dinner table. They thought it was funny. Maybe I did at the time, but today I shudder at the thought. Sometimes people go overboard with pets. We've tried not to. Members of the family, sure. Loving companions, definitely. But our children? Not quite.

From the beginning of our relationship in 1988, Charlotte and I shared a great love of animals. I learned to respect and love animals from my mother, Edith, who was raised on a farm in New Jersey. Charlotte grew up in Indianapolis with a steady collection of cats and dogs in her house. She had two cats when we started dating. I was always more attached to dogs, but Charlotte introduced me to the feline world. Her love became mine.

Topper, a brown-and-white mixed breed, had been with me since January 1984. He was a combination of collie, husky and shepherd with a circle of black fur around his left eye, just like the old "Our Gang" dog in the movies. Topper was my alter ego, a four-legged sidekick who went everywhere with me for fourteen years. He became a regular part of both my newspaper column and radio show. I signed off the broadcast every morning by saying, "Topper, get out the leash, I'm coming home." As our close friend Molly May once observed, "You can't think of Dave without automatically thinking of Topper."

Triptych, a pure white, three-legged feline, had lived with Charlotte for roughly the same amount of time. Hit by a car back in Indiana when he was just a kitten, Triptych was lucky to have survived. He was even luckier to have been adopted eventually by Charlotte. Those two enjoyed a special bond. Triptych loved to snuggle against Charlotte's chest, his left front paw on her shoulder, his head under her chin, purring and purring away. There were moments when I bordered on jealousy because of all the attention this cat received.

Thinking it was time for a new generation of pets, we decided to add Tripper in January 1995. I came up with his name as a fitting combination of Triptych and Topper. Tripper was white with huge black splotches over his body, like a cow, and a tiny Adolph Hitler black mustache. Hitler was an apt inspiration for this feline tyrant. He seemed ready to go to war with just about anyone.

Trio, a black-and-white tuxedo kitten, joined us in December 1996 as a surprise Christmas present for Charlotte, a completely spontaneous idea. Like Tripper, Trio was adopted from the North County Humane Society in nearby Atascadero, California. Wandering through the shelter's kitten room one afternoon, I looked up on the shelf where three young kittens were gathered. Trio and I made eye contact and she literally leapt off the shelf and into my arms. This would be our third cat. Trio. Keeping the "T" going just made sense at that point.

And then came Tess, the new kid, fresh from certain death at the county shelter in November 1997. It's not that we actually went looking for a second dog, but there was something special about this doomed puppy. We rescued Tess from the county shelter at the eleventh hour, barely a day before she was scheduled to be euthanized, and we took great comfort in knowing that she would now be safe because of us.

Tess deserved a chance to know love. We were never quite exactly sure of Tess's heritage. Black in coloring, we were told she was probably some type of kelpie-shepherd mix, weighing only about forty pounds. Huge ears. Small build. Big smile. She turned out to be a great dog with a sweet and gentle disposition.

Tess was a huge step for us. There was much discussion about how many pets we wanted, and how many we could handle responsibly in our small house. Five animals would certainly be a challenge.

Tess's holiday arrival was nothing less than an epiphany. When we signed off on her at the county shelter in November, Charlotte and I were really making a statement about how important pets had become in our lives. Tess made us complete. We were so happy, so blessed, to have her in our lives.

With five pets, our family turned into a four-legged Brady Bunch. Our eight-year marriage quietly reinvented itself around one shared value: No home is complete without a pet. Nor is any heart.

Another "T" joined the family. Silly us—we thought T was for luck.

Charlotte and I lived in San Luis Obispo, a town of about 40,000 people, midway between Los Angeles and San Francisco. Friendly. Clean. Safe. Plenty of trees. Great climate. Dog-friendly. The community offers a careful balance between business and environment. San Luis Obispo is home to Cal Poly State University and the colorful Madonna Inn. Hearst Castle is in the vicinity, along with Santa Barbara and Monterey. Cattle used to be big business, but now we're more interested in milking tourists.

My wife and I are both transplanted Midwesterners. I first came out here in 1987 after deciding there had to be more to life than teaching at the university level.

A series of part-time jobs around San Luis Obispo soon followed: newspaper columnist, radio talk show host, freelance writer. Charlotte moved to California from Indiana after we were married in May 1989. She's the director of public affairs and community relations for Cuesta College, the local community college. We both love the Central Coast. A day doesn't pass when we don't remark how lucky we are to live here. This is the place we were meant to be.

Together, with our animals, we lived in a small California bungalow on Pacific Street, just about a block or so from downtown San Luis Obispo. For us, it was an ideal house in an ideal location. Landlord Bill, a retired Cal Poly professor and devoted pet lover (I coined the nickname because publicity-shy Bill asked me not to use his last name in my newspaper column) had been renting us this quaint two-bedroom, 1930ish house since March 1996.

But taking Tess in made us reconsider our housing options. "Maybe it's time for us to consider moving again," Charlotte suggested. "Find a place out in the country with lots of room where we could have plenty of pets. We should think about it," she kept insisting. "Especially if we really want to have so many animals."

But the idea never germinated. Holidays are always so hectic for any type of serious decision-making. Besides, Pacific Street was such a sweet deal and rental property was tight in San Luis Obispo. Landlord Bill had owned the rental property for more than thirty years. He spent four years undertaking a complete renovation of the house, modernizing the older building while maintaining its unique historic character.

We had lived about twenty miles out in the country, in the unincorporated area of Los Osos, for the previous three years. For us, San Luis Obispo was a more vibrant and much more desirable place to live. Landlord Bill appeared equally anxious to have us in the house. He had known Charlotte for several years. He knew me through my radio show. All around, this deal seemed too good to be true.

It was a good deal—for exactly 659 days.

San Luis Obispo County Telegram-Tribune   November 7, 1997

Happy Birthday, Topper

Dear Topper,

This week officially marks your fourteenth birthday. Congratulations—that makes you ninety-eight in human years. Charlotte and I are both thrilled beyond words. We never thought this day would come.

You've been sniffing around the house all week, so let me tell you now. There's no party this year. No bone-shaped Carlock's Bakery birthday cake, no gaggle of gifts. I hope you're not too disappointed, but we opted for a quieter celebration this year. Doctor's orders. Keep things simple. Sorry, pal.

There is, however, the usual birthday steak waiting in the refrigerator. And I hope you enjoyed the bath and massage from Doggie Spa today. I think they brushed off enough fur to clothe every child in North Dakota. Oh, your buddies Quince, Lucy, Chippie, Koko, and Bonnie want you to come up to Creston and play this weekend, too. But that's about it, birthday-wise, for this year.

I was trying to think of a special gift for you, then I realized you pretty much have everything a dog needs. That's the downside of living to a ripe old age. So instead, for your birthday, I'd like to share a little story with you.

Back in January of 1984, I was returning home from visiting my parents in Chicago. I had recently started a new teaching job in a small speck-of-a-town in rural Indiana. Snow blanketed the winding two-lane, isolated, country road, already thick with ice. That didn't stop me from speeding. In those days, I was always in a hurry.

Suddenly, my car spun out of control. I glided for several hundred feet and plowed smack into a snowbank, right in front of a parked Indiana State trooper. That incident pretty much summed up my life at the time, Topper. Heading for divorce. Living in a town I hated. Doing a job I liked even less. Speeding. Out of control. Caught on thin ice.

The car was fine. I was fine. The taciturn state trooper was even cool. "What's your hurry, son?" he asked, with obvious concern.

I never lie to police officers.

Old habit. "I have to be in Crawfordsville by four o'clock," I explained. "There's a dog waiting for me at the county shelter. I need to take him home."

The story was true. I had wanted a dog for years, ever since leaving college. Jeanine, my first wife, never liked the idea. My family always advised against it. Nothing personal, Topper; they just didn't understand. But they didn't have to live in rural Indiana. I was alone, feeling miserable. It was time for a dog.

I remember calling the Indianapolis animal shelter first, but they wouldn't even talk to me since I didn't reside in the city limits. "Great!" I remember yelling into the phone. "You'll put a dog down instead of giving it to me just because of where I live!" Or in the canine vernacular, what a bunch of boneheads.

So I had to drive north to tiny Crawfordsville, to the only other animal shelter in the area. I'm sure you remember the place, Topper. A small, dumpy building with a dozen or so cages and far more than a dozen yapping dogs. My friends and I looked at every dog that day. You were the only one who didn't want to go back into the cage, the only dog who showed a spark of independence. You chose me, I swear. The shelter had a mandatory waiting period to run a background check on me. Honestly, I couldn't wait to take you home—there was never any doubt as to how great a dog you were, Topper.

I described all that earnestly to the state trooper. He must have been a dog-lover. The officer pushed me out of the snow and let me go with a stern warning and a firm handshake. "Go get that dog, son," he said. "Be good to him. Don't forget to use a leash."

That trooper understood what my family could not, and probably still doesn't. I was never meant to be a father. I was always meant to have a dog.

I'm just glad, for more reasons than you'll ever understand, that it turned out to be you. Happy Birthday, Topper. Thanks again for choosing me.

Your grateful companion,
Dave

Two

Not A Creature
Was Stirring

*T*he holiday spirit was beginning to spark in our house that Saturday before the fire. Charlotte was in a fantastic mood. She's always like a little kid around Christmas, but there was something different, something special this year. Her mother had just left after a fun and friendly visit from Indiana to celebrate her seventy-fifth birthday. Our December schedule was jammed with parties. There hadn't been a chance to do much shopping, but it didn't matter. Charlotte wasn't worried about finding lavish gifts under the tree. My wife told me that afternoon she already had everything she wanted.

"I have never been so happy, David," Charlotte whispered as we embraced in the living room by the Christmas tree. Looking around, I understood. There was Topper asleep on the couch. Tripper and Triptych snuggled together on the blue wing-back chair. Young Trio watched us curiously from her favorite perch atop the bookshelves. And seven-month-old Tess, the new puppy, stood at our feet, furiously trying to wedge herself between us, demanding attention. Again. Charlotte dashed into the other room, quickly returning with her camera. "Let's get some pictures," she suggested.

I hastily scooped up the cats and placed them on the living room sofa, three-legged Triptych on the right arm. Tripper and Trio on the back. Lethargic Topper was already at home on the couch—he reluctantly shifted down to make room for an overly enthusiastic Tess. Five pets staring in five different directions; none of them especially happy to be posed this close to each other.

"Stay...stay," I kept coaxing the dogs.

"Ready...here we go," warned Charlotte as she took aim. Click-Click-Click. Three flashes. Three photos. All five pets together in an informal holiday portrait.

The minute Charlotte put down the camera, our animals sped off, except Topper, who at fourteen, was much too lazy to move for anything. He stayed on the sofa, a canine couch potato, quite content to remain horizontal.

Charlotte sounded equally satisfied. "I got some good shots. Hope they turn out OK."

There were two holiday parties scheduled for that weekend. On Saturday night, December 13, my newspaper editor John Moore opened up his San Luis Obispo home for a staff party. The following night was the KVEC radio Christmas party scheduled, as per tradition, for McLintock's Steak House in nearby Shell Beach.

Neither Charlotte nor I are much for the party circuit. With all of our pets, we had become real "homebodies," not interested in going out unless it was something very special. Besides, the Christmas decorations needed to be finished and we were still recovering from all the excitement of my mother-in-law's recent visit.

And, of course, there was Topper. He had slowed down considerably in recent months as the arthritis spread through his hips and back. The clock was ticking. Would it be weeks? Months? No one knew. Even thinking about life without Topper was difficult, so Charlotte and I really hadn't made any firm plans for dealing with those final days. Our primary goal was to make sure that no matter what, Topper didn't suffer. We owed him that much.

Two consecutive nights of socializing did not top our list of priorities. The newspaper folks could party without us. Instead, we chose to go to the KVEC dinner on Sunday night and keep things simple since we both had to work the next day. Actually, I had a newspaper column to finish before Monday morning, so there was even more reason not to be away too long.

My column for Tuesday, December 16, was to be special. No doubt motivated by our positive experience with young Tess, I planned a new holiday tradition for the newspaper. Each December, I decided, there would be one entire column devoted to publishing a list of dogs and cats who were available for adoption from the county shelter. That would be my annual Christmas gift to the animals at the shelter—a chance for some of them to get the gift of life. I had already made arrangements with county animal control officer Geoff Clinton to email me an up-to-date shelter list that Sunday afternoon.

Sitting down at my computer in our combination office/spare bedroom, I put together the opening as I waited to hear from Geoff. Under the proposed headline, "The Gift That Keeps on Giving," I began:

> I do this for Topper and Tess, and for Triptych and Tripper and Trio, as well. I do this because Christmas is approaching, and I've been taught that it is always better to give than to receive.
>
> And I do this because earlier this month President Clinton received a new dog, a $5000 pure-bred puppy. Good for you, Mr. President, but there are currently several thousand unwanted dogs across the country who will never live to see Christmas morning. Wasn't there room for one of them—just one—at the White House?

That's as far as I got. Geoff had agreed to send me more specific details about the dogs and cats on his wish list. Another email would be waiting when we returned from the KVEC party. I felt excited and pleased about Tuesday's column, hoping somehow it might help. "It's worth it if just one dog or cat gets rescued from this," I told Charlotte. "I'll settle for one."

December typically brings rain to the Central Coast and El Niño was beginning. Plenty of rain had already fallen in the first part of the month. I liked to take Topper and Tess to nearby Laguna Lake Park a few times each day. We were there that Sunday morning, and again that afternoon. The contrast between the two dogs was dramatic. Tess, so full of energy and excitement, Topper so slow and tired. Tess always deferred to her elder and Topper seemed to tolerate, however warily, this kinetic newcomer.

On our last Sunday together, the ground was especially wet and soggy. I kept both walks short and simple. Topper in particular never did like to get wet. He hated anything involving water. When he was a puppy back in Indiana, the animal control officer supposedly found him hiding under a porch trying to escape the rain. On the other hand, Tess didn't care about getting wet. I don't think anything ever bothered her.

Shortly after 6p.m., dressed casually for the radio dinner, I took Topper and Tess out for one last excursion, a brief on-leash jaunt through Emerson Park, just down the street from our house. Despite the soggy weather, the dogs needed to get out before we left. For some strange reason, I toyed with the idea of taking Tess with us to the dinner and leaving her in the car to see how she would behave. Besides, a puppy in the car might be a good excuse to leave early. I decided against it, in part because of the cold night air and the chance of more rain.

Cocktails began at 7 p.m., with dinner at 8. Our strategy was to arrive somewhere around 7:30. We were in no hurry to leave the house. We turned off the TV. Took one last turn in front of the mirror. Checked for our keys. Left some lights on. Same old routine. I stood in the open front doorway, waiting for Charlotte. Topper, sensing that he wasn't coming along, staked out the couch. Triptych, Tripper, and Trio were already spread out above him. Only Tess didn't understand and she made an anxious dash for the door.

"No, stay," I said, pointing to the couch. She obeyed, settling in reluctantly next to Topper. "Good dog, Tess."

I watched as Charlotte took the time to say goodbye to all five. She always did that, never leaving the house until she knew where all the pets were, and that they were safe. Charlotte spent time with each one, working the couch like a politician working a crowd. "You'll behave, Topper, won't you?" "And here's my Triptych, my little Triptych." Each of the five got special attention, a little kiss or an affectionate scratch behind the ear. Only then could Charlotte leave satisfied.

Not a creature was stirring that holiday night. All seemed quiet and normal, the five settled on the couch for the night.

"We'll be back," I promised, just as I always did every time we walked out the front door. "Try and stay out of trouble." Then we shut and locked the front door behind us, sealing their fate.

There was absolutely no reason for alarm that night. No second thought to any of our actions. But only with 20/20 hindsight could we realize our oversight—neither one of us remembered to check the thermostat in the back hallway.

California in December, compared to Midwest winters, really doesn't get that cold, but cold enough. Many people in Central California have their furnaces turned on regularly from November through February.

Charlotte is especially adverse to cold weather, so we tend to keep our house rather toasty during the winter months. Landlord Bill had renovated the house, but the heating system stayed pretty much the same—a gas furnace in the basement shooting up heat through one main floor grill in the rear of the living room. One of the reasons our pets tended to hover around the sofa was the close proximity to the warm air.

Charlotte and I always, *always* turned the heat off when we left. Always, except for that night—Sunday, December 14, 1997—for reasons that we will never be able to understand.

We were gone three hours. That's how little time it took.

San Luis Obispo County Telegram-Tribune   *August 22, 1997*

The Great Cat Escape

As I write this, I can hear our three-legged cat Triptych nearby in the kitchen, helping himself to a late-night snack. The little bell around his collar bangs up against the white porcelain bowl as he eats. It's a comforting, reassuring sound.

Charlotte and I have tried to reach an understanding with our cats. We promise to feed, love, and spoil them. They have the complete run of the house. We ask only one thing in return (two, if you count the litter box): We expect our cats to remain indoors.

The cats never venture outside. It's a jungle out there, we warn, as if they ever listen. Too many cars, too many dogs, and far too much danger. Certainly no place for a defenseless kitty-cat.

But boys will be boys and cats will be cats. It's that curiosity thing they share. We know, especially after the other night. Charlotte and I were both asleep—it took only a second to jump from a dream to a nightmare.

I heard our neighbor Jackie gently rapping on the back door, urgently calling out to us. The digital clock on the nightstand read 3:30. Charlotte and I stumbled out of bed, without a clue as to what was happening. Jackie had horrible news—Triptych and Tripper had gone AWOL (Absent Without Official Leash).

Sure enough, the window in the spare bedroom had been left partially open due to the recent sweltering summer heat. More than enough space for a pair of crafty, conniving cats, feline felons, to sneak through, paw out the screen and leap to freedom in the backyard. Our youngest cat Trio was either too chicken or too smart; she stayed behind, perhaps as a decoy.

Triptych and Tripper, however, started celebrating just a bit too soon. All their gleeful racket stirred Jackie, a fellow cat lover, from her bed. She threw on her robe and ran to investigate.

What followed next was more like a scene from a Keystone Cop comedy: Jackie spies Tripper in the yard. Jackie grabs Tripper. Tripper hisses. Jackie hangs on to Tripper. Tripper scratches Jackie. Jackie hangs on valiantly. Triptych freaks out in response to ruckus. A badly scratched Jackie forces a most-angry Tripper back through the bedroom window. A disoriented Triptych bolts for the bushes in the dead of night.

One cat recovered. One three-legged cat still on the run. Actor Tommy Lee Jones pops to mind suddenly and I start hearing his speech to the deputies in *The Fugitive* after Harrison Ford escapes.

"All right, listen up! We have an unarmed escapee who's been on the run for ten minutes. That's one-two-*three* city blocks. I want a complete house-to-house search. Every farmhouse. Every outhouse. And especially every cathouse. Your fugitive's name is Triptych."

But Charlotte is far from smiling. Nothing in this world—nothing—means more to her than that three-legged ball of white fur. There is no response as she calls out urgently and repeatedly to Triptych, no reassuring sound of the little bell on his collar. I can't see my wife's face in the darkness. I don't need to. The concern in her cracking voice speaks volumes.

Topper, meanwhile, remains calmly stretched out on the kitchen floor, refusing to budge, to show even a biscuit of concern over a missing cat. Stepping over him, I grab our flashlight. The batteries hardly work; the tiny light flickers on and off, losing power by the second.

Jackie, Charlotte, and I swing into action; combing the nearby backyards, hoping no nervous neighbor accidentally opens fire as we check under porches and crouch down by bushes. Given the hour, the streets are thankfully empty, but there is no sign of poor Triptych, a frightened cat, a complete stranger to this post-midnight, cold, outside world.

A half-hour passes. Nothing. No bells, no meows. Charlotte shines the erratic light under some steps that block a narrow alley. She catches a brief glimpse of the tip of a white tail dashing into a small hole in the foundation of a house. It's either Triptych or the beginning of Charlotte in Wonderland.

My wife can't squeeze around the narrow steps. She has to circle the house and leap over some bushes to get anywhere near the opening. There is no hesitation. On her hands and knees in the dirt at four in the morning, Charlotte gently-oh-so-gently tries to coax Triptych outside. He won't budge.

Instead, the cat exits out still another hole in the foundation and makes a beeline for the front door of our house. Smart cat. Out of breath, Charlotte finally catches her cat, scooping him up lovingly in her arms and carries him back into the safety of our house. I round up Topper, Trio, and the still-indignant Tripper.

Unable to sleep, we all sit quietly together in the living room for the next hour, or so, letting the drama sink in, the moment pass.

Safe and warm. Together again in The Great Indoors.

THREE

The Night That Will Last Forever

*D*eath is a relative stranger who had kept his distance from me. I never knew my grandparents. Mom and Dad are still living. My father-in-law died before I met Charlotte. Aunts and uncles were merely long-distance voices on the telephone and their passing meant nothing to me. I had been to a grand total of one funeral, a girlfriend's grandfather, in the first forty-two years of my life.

That began to change. The editor of my newspaper was killed along with his wife and a daughter in a horrific car accident in November 1995. We had just been together the day before. Then our congressman, Walter Capps, died of a heart attack in October 1997, slightly more than a week after he had appeared on my radio show.

Meanwhile, my close friend, Mike Veron, only fifty-two years old, faced a spreading cancer. My hope remained that somehow he'd make it to fifty-three. Watching his gradual but steady decline became increasingly difficult. We didn't know if Mike or Topper would go first, but we were clearly in the eleventh hour for both and trying to be strong.

Of course, we had no idea how our lives were about to change. That Sunday night Charlotte and I were more concerned with just trying to stay awake during the staid radio station dinner. Deliberately seated at the far back table in the small banquet room, we didn't socialize too much, and fortunately, drank even less.

About thirty minutes into the dinner, KVEC general manager Dan Clarkson, a fifty-something teddy bear, collapsed on the floor. He had been drinking on an empty stomach and his body, still recovering from a bout with the flu, obviously did not approve. Paramedics arrived and a conscious but rather embarrassed Danny was rolled away to the hospital to raucous cheers and applause. Everyone thought this had been the evening's excitement. Little did we know.

Things began to wind down just before 10 p.m. Charlotte and I shared one of those "let's-get-out-of-here" stares as we maneuvered towards the exit amid the last round of holiday hugs and cheer. I felt anxious to get home and finish my newspaper column. Charlotte just wanted to be home.

The drive along Highway 101 from Shell Beach to San Luis Obispo takes less than ten minutes. Charlotte and I talked about the dinner, mostly laughing about Dan Clarkson's sudden departure and what I could say about it the next morning on my radio show. We swung off the Marsh Street exit. Up two blocks. Right on Beach Street. One block over to Pacific Street. Turn right. There's home. How many times had we made this drive?

However, this time when we turned that final corner, we turned a new corner in our lives. It only took a few seconds. One minute everything was fine, and the next, the walls came crashing down, suddenly, instantly, without warning.

As I pulled up along the curb, Charlotte was the first to notice something wrong. "The lights aren't on," she said, looking at our house. Her voice took an anxious turn. "I think I see smoke."

From this moment on, everything happened in some sort of surrealistic daze at three-quarters time. The normally lighted house was indeed dark. There was indeed smoke sifting out. We bolted from the car and rushed towards the front door.

Nervously, I unlocked the door, which opens directly into the living room. Topper and Tess normally greeted us. Tonight there was nothing but an eerie silence. Inside, the house was pitch black. A gust of smoke rushed towards our faces and flames shot up from the basement in the back of the house. My stomach knotted as I called out for the animals. "Topper! Tess! Tripper!" Nothing. The increasing smoke forced us back out to the front patio area. I pulled the front door shut.

"Go call 9-1-1!" I yelled. Charlotte hesitated for just a second. We were both so overwhelmed by the moment. "Go!" I urged again. Charlotte ran towards the neighbor's house. Behind me were the double windows that faced into the dining room. I broke out a window with my wrists. I had to see inside.

Squinting through the haze. I could see Topper's lifeless form sprawled out on the tiled floor, just next to the dining room table. That moment will remain with me forever. I knew then we had lost all five.

After Charlotte ran off to call for help, I began shouting. "Help! Please help! Fire! Fire!" I broke open more windows with the palm of my hands and wrists, hoping that I could see inside and hoping beyond hope a frightened Triptych or Tess would come scampering out into my arms. Maybe I was trying to draw the smoke out. I can't explain. I lost all sense of time and space. Some type of strange inertia seemed to propel me into action, some of it helpful, some irrational.

The nauseous, rancid odor of the fumes was overpowering. Common sense dictated that we stand back and wait for the fire department, but any rational thought vanished the second I recognized Topper through the broken dining room window. Hunched over, I forced my way through the front door and into the dining room. I scooped up all eighty pounds of a limp Topper and carried him outside. Carefully, I placed him on the sidewalk as the shock of his lifeless body in my arms began to register.

Long after the horror of this night ended, I would take great personal satisfaction in knowing that I was the one who found Topper, the one who brought him out of the fire. I had long prepared myself for the moment when I would gently hold a dead Topper in my arms and say farewell. But not like this.

Immediately, I wondered if I could give CPR to a dog. That's how desperate I felt, grasping at anything as I huddled over my dog's lifeless body. Then reality quickly kicked in. Topper was gone. Every ounce of energy had been drained from his body. There was no time to grieve or reflect. Something else was controlling me now, pushing me forward. Where were the other four? Maybe, just maybe, there was a chance.

So back inside I went, crawling on my hands and knees to avoid the fumes. The flames remained at the rear of the house. I never felt at serious risk, though given my frame of mind personal safety wasn't the issue. Groping frantically about the living room, I came across the limp body of a cat lying under the coffee table, directly in front of the couch.

Too little light and too much smoke made it impossible to identify the cat. All I could do was clutch the furry body close to my chest and dash outside. My heart sank as I stood on the front porch, finally able to see that I was holding Triptych, Charlotte's beloved three-legged cat. First Topper, now Triptych. In only a matter of minutes, this had become a living nightmare.

Meanwhile, an equally concerned and determined Charlotte tried to get in through the back door. She managed to get as far as the kitchen sink where she found the body of Tripper stretched out on the linoleum floor. The overpowering fumes quickly chased her back, but not before she was able to retrieve Tripper.

The increasing intensity of the fire made more trips inside the house impossible. Sirens wailed in the night, speeding in our direction.

Firefighters would have to find Tess and Trio. The grim realization kept hitting me that they would be looking for bodies, not live animals. Dead or alive, we wanted our animals accounted for and someone had to reach them before the flames did.

The San Luis Obispo Fire Department quickly had the fire under control. They were able to keep the flames confined to the rear of the house. There didn't seem to be any damage on the exterior, or to the overall structure.

In the initial chaos, I was surprised to see a familiar face in uniform. Our friend Jerry James happened to be on duty. Jerry would be an important lifeline during the night, making it easier for us to communicate with officials and offering a steady hand through our early trauma. The immediate concern I expressed to Jerry was to locate Tess and Trio.

Going in through the back door, it didn't take the firefighters long. They brought out the two remaining bodies. As overcome with grief as I was at the time, I did feel a moment of relief. All five animals had been found. All five bodies were out of the house. One small hollow victory.

I took Tess from the firefighters and laid her next to Topper on the sidewalk. Jerry told me that the two dogs would have to be moved because they were in the way. I lifted up each of them and moved them over to the corner of the driveway. A small but growing crowd from the neighborhood began gathering across the street, watching us in curious silence.

My red, weathered Toyota pickup truck was parked on the street, directly in front of the house. Charlotte took Triptych, Tripper, and Trio and placed them next to one another on the front seat. They were covered with soot, their bodies permeated with the stench of fire. Any feeling of satisfaction I had from getting them out of the house was quickly lost when I saw those five bodies. The shock to my system continued to mount.

Charlotte and I began a strange dance. It seemed important that we stay connected to each other throughout all this. We kept running over and embracing each other, trying our best to comfort and explain that which could never be explained. Nothing we said or did could hold back the flood of tears.

"Listen to me!" I blurted out, pressing Charlotte closer to me. "They didn't burn, OK? We got them out of there, right? Right?"

"But why all five, David?" Charlotte demanded to know. "Why Topper and Tripper and Triptych and…. Her cracking voice trailed off, unable to finish. I didn't have an answer.

When we weren't with each other, we were with our animals. Moving back and forth between the two dogs in the driveway and the three cats in the truck. I knelt down by both Topper and Tess, taking turns holding and petting them. "I am so sorry, Topper. Tess, I'm so sorry," I wailed repeatedly. "It's going to be OK. It's going to be OK. Charlotte and I are here. We're so sorry for leaving you tonight."

Their lifeless bodies were silent in the face of my encouragement, which only compounded the grief. Then I ran over to the truck, opened the door and leaned down by Tripper, Triptych and Trio on the seat. I petted each one and gently held them in my arms. More tears. More apologies. *I'm sorry…. I'm so sorry.*

Our neighbor Carol became one of many angels that night. A dog lover, she was close to her own dog, Brandy. Carol was visibly upset by what was happening. She kept asking what she could do to help, so I asked her to call our veterinarian, Dr. Richard Knighton, and alert him as to what had happened. Dr. Knighton didn't hesitate to drive the fifteen miles into town from his home at 10:30 at night. He would come as soon as possible along with his wife and fellow veterinarian, Dr. Susan Choy.

While waiting for the veterinarians to arrive, Charlotte and I hovered protectively around our animals. No one was to touch them. Whatever happened to the house, happened. We didn't care about our personal belongings. We stayed close to our five pets, making sure they were safe, even in death.

Other people had to be notified, especially my elderly parents in Seattle. Yet there was no way I could make that call. Mom would be devastated over the loss of Topper. Both parents would worry about us. Instead, using Carol's cellular phone, I called my older brother, Bob, in Los Angeles and explained the situation. "I need you to tell Mom and Dad," I explained. "Make sure Mom understands that they didn't suffer. That's very important. They didn't suffer." Bob said he'd handle things. He always did.

The media side of me insisted on another call, this time to the radio station. After all, KVEC was the news/talk station in town. News director Suzan Vaughn would need to know and she deserved to hear it from me directly. I also called two of our closest friends, Jim and Eileen, who lived about thirty minutes away. Their three young boys loved our pets. All of us had just been together for Thanksgiving at our house. I wanted them to hear what happened directly from me, not the media. Jim answered the phone.

"There's been a terrible fire, Jim!" I screamed above the fire engines. "The animals are dead. They're all dead!"

The response was laughter on the other end. Jim, ever the jokester, thought I was trying to pull one over on him.

"Hey, man. Have you been drinking?" he asked, still laughing. He wouldn't believe me, despite my furious protests to the contrary. Angry, I gave up and handed the phone to Charlotte.

Our introduction to grief counseling came in the form of the police chaplain on duty that night. On staff at one of the local mortuaries, he was a volunteer, on-call chaplain. His job was to console, but I quickly realized that he knew nothing about grieving. He was bound and determined to chase away my pain. Instead of listening, the police chaplain insisted on telling me how I should be feeling. Sounding as sincere and friendly as the firefighters, he seemed clueless as to the importance of grieving and emotional release.

Casually, he slipped his arm around my shoulder as I stood over the bodies of Topper and Tess. He mustered up every possible ounce of sincerity and said, "Look, I know how you feel, Dave."

Then it got worse. "Yeah, I had a German shepherd," the police chaplain continued earnestly. "Two years ago, I had to put him down. He was in my arms. It was really tough."

Engulfed in the horror of the last thirty minutes, I stood motionless, surrounded by our five dead animal companions. This man's words, however well-intended, rang empty, void of any understanding of the extent of our loss. Speechless, my only choice was to ignore him. He persisted in recounting the story of his dog. I just wanted him to go away.

Yet another part of me wanted to grab this joker and lean into his face and say, "Let me tell you something—you have no idea of how I feel right now! You have no clue unless you've ever come home to find your house on fire and five animals that you loved beyond words lying dead at your feet, including one that was less than a year old. And another who's been with me for fourteen years. But I don't get to say goodbye to him—to any of them, do I? I don't particularly give a damn about how you're feeling, pal. Don't even try to pretend you understand what's happening here."

Instead, I stomped over to Jerry and begged him to please get rid of that guy before I punched someone in the nose. Meanwhile, the hapless chaplain tried a similar spiel on Charlotte, serving only to aggravate her even more. She also turned away from him.

The chaplain went home early that night. In the aftermath of the tragedy, I would try repeatedly to forget his face, his name, his very existence. His attempt to express sympathy was only the first of some awkward attempts by individuals who tried to express sympathy, but ended up sounding hurtful. People felt the need to respond by comparing our loss to something they had lost. As we quickly learned that first night, sometimes it's better not to say anything at all.

The firefighters kept urging us to leave. They especially wanted me to go to the hospital and have a doctor examine my hands. I suspect their larger concern was getting us away from the scene as quickly as possible. Now, I wonder how many of them had pets of their own. How many of those firefighters that night had a sense of what Charlotte and I were going through? Regardless, we refused to leave. Our tone was cooperative, but adamant. Charlotte and I weren't going anywhere until Dr. Knighton arrived to take care of our pets. The subject wasn't open for debate.

As we waited, the rain returned, a steady drizzle. Tess and Topper were still stretched out at the end of the driveway. One of the firefighters was kind enough to give me a yellow tarp to cover their bodies.

I became a human pinball, bouncing from Jerry if he had questions, to Charlotte for a supportive hug, back to the truck to be with Triptych, Trio and Tripper, over to the sidewalk to kneel down with Topper and Tess. Bystanders continued to crowd Pacific Street, but I felt completely alone.

The tears and rain became one. I couldn't stop crying. I kept talking to each one of our animal companions, repeating how much we loved them and how sorry we felt for what had happened. I wrapped my arms around Topper and buried my face in his body, my voice muffled with equal doses of apology and love. "You're the best dog, Topper. I swear, there's never been a better dog. There never will be a better dog."

Holding Topper in my arms in the rain only fueled my growing bewilderment and the numbing frustration building inside me. Everything just became too much for me to handle. I looked towards the sky and began yelling angrily.

"Couldn't you have spared just one?" I kept babbling. "Would that be asking too much? Just one of them? Couldn't you have left us one?" Bystanders stared at me. I didn't care. I just continued yelling. Charlotte hurried over to embrace me, trying to calm me down.

Local television news crews arrived on the scene, but we ignored the cameras. Fortunately, they respected our privacy and kept their distance. Clearly, Charlotte and I were in no mood to talk.

Landlord Bill and his entire family soon appeared on the scene. There was nothing anyone could say. Charlotte and I felt such guilt because the house Bill had worked so hard to restore now stood ravaged. But he would hear none of it. That night his heart and mind weighed solely on our loss. Bill stood stoically in the drizzle, puffing on that worn pipe of his, missing Topper and the others already as if they had been his own.

Dr. Knighton and Dr. Choy finally arrived. They ran separate veterinary practices in Los Osos and we took our pets to Rich Knighton, but we had also gotten to know Susan over the years. Both were highly regarded practitioners who once again showed that they were willing, literally, to go the extra mile for us.

Rich is a straight-arrow guy, decidedly low-key, rarely excitable. But even the darkness couldn't mask the heartfelt anguish and clear distraught in his eyes.

"I'm so sorry. I'm so sorry," was all he could say as we embraced in the rain.

Susan wrapped her arms around Charlotte and then tried to comfort me. "Thank you. Thanks so much for coming," I mumbled through another wave of tears, digging my fingers into Susan's back, overwhelmed with a strong sense of relief because our veterinarians had arrived. What a stark contrast to our recent run-in with the chaplain. Rich and Susan were pet people whom we could trust. They understood. They would do the right thing for our animals.

"Take your time tonight," Rich encouraged. "We'll wait."

But there was nothing to wait for. Topper, Triptych, Tripper, Trio, and Tess were dead. With the fire under control, the firefighters appeared eager to leave and even more eager for us to leave. There seemed little point in prolonging the nightmare.

So even as the fog of disbelief lingered, Charlotte and I made one last round in the rain, saying a final goodbye, offering one last round of apologies to our animals. A kiss. A hug. More tears for each one. When there were no more good-byes left, Rich and Susan wrapped each of the bodies in separate blankets and carefully placed them in the back of their sport utility vehicle. Charlotte and I embraced as we stood in the middle of Pacific Street, watching the tail lights disappear in the rain, taking all that we loved out of harm's way forever.

With our animals gone, we had to decide what to do next. Fortunately, our good friends Bob and Janna Nichols were in town. Janna was Charlotte's closest friend—they met for coffee every Saturday morning. When they received Charlotte's call, they rushed right over and insisted we stay at their house.

So shortly after midnight, we thanked the remaining firefighters profusely for all their hard work. Then Janna drove us to Sierra Vista Regional Medical Center in San Luis Obispo. Little was said during the short drive to the hospital.

Still in shock, we were running on empty. The hospital emergency room was practically deserted with only a skeleton staff going about their routine. What a stark contrast to the emotional chaos we had just left on Pacific Street.

Charlotte had a minor cut on her right hand. There were six separate lacerations on my wrists and lower palms, including an inch-long gash on my right wrist, the result of breaking out windows. The nurse on duty asked me to lie down and she started an IV immediately.

To my surprise, a familiar face strolled through the double doors. The doctor on duty, Steve Sainsbury, had been a guest on my radio show several times. Charlotte calmly explained the situation. Dr.

Sainsbury immediately pulled the ER staff together, and with great compassion explained, "This couple lost their family tonight. It would be like you losing your children."

He was right, but I had no more tears left. I just felt emotionally drained. Supportive emergency room nurses cleaned and sutured my cuts before wrapping my wrists in bandages. The doctor gave each of us a mild sedative to help us sleep. After that, we were released and Janna drove us to her house.

We stumbled into their guest room well past 1 a.m. with little more than the clothes on our back and a packet of sedatives. Grateful for the sanctuary, we still felt awkward about intruding on friends during the hectic holiday season. Bob and Janna were expecting family members home for the holidays, but that didn't matter to them at the moment. They made us their complete focus.

Neither Charlotte nor I knew exactly how to respond. How quickly we had jumped from heaven to hell. On Saturday, we had never been happier. Never. By late Sunday night, our lives fell apart completely. The best we could do was huddle quietly under the covers and pray the sedatives would reach us before the nightmares. Thankfully, they did.

San Luis Obispo County Telegram - Tribune December 5, 1997

Regarding Tess

She's smart. A good listener, but not afraid to speak up. Nice long legs. Soft, smooth skin. Dark-brown eyes. Energetic. Fun-loving. Spontaneous. She makes me feel young again.

Her name is Tess and we've been seen together around town a lot lately. Openly affectionate with each other. I don't care. This is true love, no mere casual fling. Honest. Charlotte wisely doesn't try to interfere. She knows better than to force me to choose.

But Topper? The poor dog is silently fuming in anger, stunned by my sudden betrayal. I have done the unthinkable to my loyal companion of fourteen years. I have brought another dog home. Actually, Tess is barely seven months old; strictly a case of puppy love that my grumpy older dog simply refuses to acknowledge.

For the last three years, friends and even complete strangers have been suggesting that we add a second dog to the family. I have always resisted. That wouldn't be fair to Topper, I typically argued.

Besides, I don't have the strength to make that emotional commitment to another animal. When Topper goes, that's it.

No more. Move on.

But as any experienced pet lover knows, we don't choose pets. They choose us. Charlotte and I never really knew what hit us. A friend had adopted a young puppy as a surprise gift for his wife. Then the wife gave my friend a sur-prise—divorce papers. The poor dog became caught in the middle. My friend no longer wanted the dog; he decided reluctantly to turn her in to the county pound.

There are those moments in life for which there are no clear explanations; times in which the heart acts faster than the brain. Seeing Tess was one of those rare moments. This black dog has no unique markings. She's just a little mutt like the thousands of other homeless mutts who are destroyed every year. But when Tess trotted across the shelter parking lot and nuzzled her snout in my arms, something clicked.

So Charlotte and I decided to take Tess in and try to find her a loving home. We called friend after friend. No luck. Everyone had a legitimate excuse. Everyone was already too busy with the holidays to worry about the plight of a single homeless dog. I was quickly running out of people to call. There had to be somebody, somewhere.

Meanwhile, Tess played us with the shrewdness of a carnival midway barker. She knew all the right buttons to push. I woke up in the middle of the night once to find her snuggled next to me—I thought it was Charlotte. She was completely house-trained in less than three days. Good dog. She came when called. Very good dog. She barked at night if she heard footsteps outside. Excellent dog.

As the days went by, we quietly accepted the inevitable. Tess belonged here, with us. Of course, we don't love Topper any less. No pet will ever replace him.

But being with Tess also made me realize that our love and commitment to animals can't die with Topper. Unfortunately, there are others who need what Charlotte and I have to offer. The circle must continue.

Landlord Bill signed off on Tess immediately. I suspect he's going to spoil her, too. Having this second dog has already brought a new layer of warmth into our house. There's something very satisfying from going room to room and finding a dog or cat sound asleep, safe and warm. And knowing that you made that possible.

Now all I have to do is work on Topper, who still shows his displeasure daily. The puppy always wants to play. The grizzled veteran wants none of it. Topper is quick to establish his territory in both the truck and the house. He's not afraid to snap at Tess if she gets in his way, or sneaks at his food. And that sad look in his eyes, the "how-could-you-Dave?" stare of disbelief.

Sorry, Topper. There was nothing I could do. I was chosen. And, like you, I had to obey.

FOUR

I Didn't Know If I Should Wait

*T*he morning after the fire I awoke with the dawn, immediately sensing something different. Charlotte and I were accustomed to waking up to our pets. Who needed an alarm clock when you have three cats and two dogs? Triptych, Tripper and Trio tended to give poor Charlotte only until around 6 a.m. to wake up. After that, they smothered her, three little purr machines lurking like vultures. Demanding breakfast, they surrounded her. *Wake up, Charlotte. We're hungry! Why are your eyes closed? Can't you hear us, Charlotte? Charlotte? Charlotte? Wake up, please?*

Topper and Tess tended to be only slightly more subtle, resorting to a mere paw up on the bed, always on my side. Not that they were hungry. They could eat later. Topper and Tess just needed to get outside for a little relief. Quick!

That daily routine made mornings special on Pacific Street, even at that early hour. All seven of us were rarely together in the same room, otherwise. We woke up to them. Started our day with them. They gave us a reason to march out the door and face the human world.

But not today. That first Monday morning, I awoke to the all-too-quiet, empty, guest bedroom. The silence was deafening. No cats. No dogs. No purring. No friendly paws. Nothing.

Laying awake in bed, my eyes darted around the room, half-expecting to see Triptych leap up on Charlotte's side, followed by Tripper and Trio. Where are the dogs? Don't they need to go out? Maybe last night was all just a horrible dream, but no, as my bandaged wrists reminded me, no dream.

So there I lay, the proverbial stranger in a strange land. That queasy feeling in my stomach returned. I reached for the phone. *Time to get busy*, I told myself. *Stay busy.*

First would be the phone calls to friends around town and around the country. Although I didn't particularly feel like talking to anyone, I felt compelled to let people know about the fire and the loss of our pets. *They needed to know. Just keep the conversation short.*

"I have some bad news," I'd announce. "This is what happened.... Yes, all five. No, the pets just went to sleep. They didn't burn. Charlotte and I are safe.... We're OK...really. We'll let you know what we decide to do next. Yeah.... Merry Christmas."

Our friends were stunned by the news. Some had known Topper since his puppy days. Their voices cracked and conversations were punctuated by awkward silences as they struggled to offer some level of comfort. Yet there was really nothing they could say. They knew it. I knew it. *Keep it short. Move on, Dave.* Charlotte and I learned quickly that it was important to keep moving, especially in those early morning hours when the grief felt strongest.

Meanwhile, word of the fire spread rapidly around town. The television station carried footage from Sunday night on its 6:30 a.m. Monday newscast, incorrectly reporting that two of the pets had survived. KVEC also gave the story prime coverage during the morning drive time block, based largely on my brief Sunday night voice mail message. Loyal station listeners soon began calling KVEC in disbelief. The messages would continue nonstop all week.

My radio talk show airs weekday mornings from 10:05 until 12 noon on a small AM station, broadcasting from downtown San Luis

Obispo. Don Imus, I ain't, but we try to cover what's happening locally in the community. Listeners know me. They know how much Topper and the other animals meant to us. When my theme music played at 10:05, news director Suzan Vaughn took the microphone. My scheduled segments had been cancelled, Suzan explained. I would be away indefinitely.

Instead, Suzan devoted the entire two hours to letting people know about the fire and giving them a chance to call in. Joining her for part of the discussion were Angelo Procopio, who worked part-time at the station, along with our popular state senator Jack O'Connell. Jack's district office was less than a block from the radio station. He knew Charlotte and me. He had also met Topper on several occasions. When Jack heard the news, he rushed directly to the station. No showboating here, it's just the kind of decent community-oriented guy he is.

The news of our loss seemed particularly tough for Angelo because he had been through a devastating fire himself only a few years prior. Obviously painful memories stirred in Angelo's voice as he talked about our fire.

"There's a phase-out that they're going to have to go through," Angelo explained. "You just can't deal with anything right off the bat. There's a numbness that happens and you just have to go through this period. You could have all the insurance in the world. It doesn't matter— it doesn't compensate the feelings. You've just lost everything that was your life, that surrounded your life, and you're just left standing."

Angelo added, "I'd caution Dave and Charlotte not to have any guilt feelings, like it's something they did. That fire just happened. It's not you. A lot of times we want to say, 'What did I do? What could I have done to avoid this?' Probably nothing. It's just something that happens."

During the course of the discussion, Senator O'Connell added, "Dave and Charlotte are two very strong people. They had a tremendous love and affection for those animals. Both of them are very active in the animal rescue movement here in town, throughout the whole county. I'm sure they're feeling a real loss this morning."

We were—far too much to listen to the radio. Charlotte and I talked that morning, huddled together behind the closed, guest bedroom door, still in shock. Our immediate priority was to salvage what we could from the house and to vacate Pacific Street as quickly as possible. We needed distance from the tragedy.

Wanting to stay busy and feeling some sense of obligation, I offered to supervise the move. "There's no need for you to go back. There's no need for you to ever go inside that house again," I told Charlotte. "I'll take care of it." She didn't want to go back, so we made a deal. I would get us out of the old house while Charlotte found us a new place to live.

I didn't even bother to take a shower. After throwing on some borrowed clothes, I headed directly for the house. The rain had stopped, replaced by a crisp, sunny December morning. Pacific Street was quiet, a marked contrast to the chaos of the night before. Landlord Bill's truck was parked on the street. All the broken front windows had been boarded up.

A large white banner with red lettering taped across the front door immediately caught my eye, *David & Charlotte, We All Love You!* Red roses had been placed at the base of the door. I sighed, the first of many that day. It was going to be a long morning.

Damage to the exterior structure was basically negligible. Inside, however, was a much different story. Everything seemed just as we had left it before the KVEC party, but with a most obvious difference. More than one person would tell me that they had never seen smoke penetrate furniture and walls so extensively. Nothing had been spared. Books. Linens. Silverware. Dishes. Holiday decorations. Christmas cards. Picture frames. Cosmetics. Computer equipment. Wrapped presents. All blanketed in ash and soot. The dank stench hung in the air.

Firefighters had partially ripped up the flooring in the rear hallway that connected the bathroom and two back bedrooms. Standing in the living room, close to where Charlotte had so warmly embraced me just forty-eight hours earlier, I now had a clear shot through a gaping hole in the wooden floor down into the basement and what was left of the furnace.

Seeing everything in the light of day only reinforced how lucky we had been overall that the house didn't completely burn to the ground. Given the sheer power of the fumes, I understood that our animals never had a chance. No, there was nothing we could have done.

Silently, I struggled to maintain my composure as the true extent of damage began to register. Picking my way from room to room, one overwhelming concern started to haunt me. *Did I cause this? Is this my fault? Was I the one who left the furnace on? Or was it Charlotte?*

The issue kept dogging me all morning, especially as I uncovered more damage to personal possessions. As friends began streaming by to offer their condolences, I tried to shake off the images of dead pets. Each time, I questioned if this nightmare was from my own negligence. I told myself I could never face Charlotte if I had carelessly caused Triptych's death. She knew I felt the same way about Topper.

There would never be an answer to that question. It doesn't matter. Angelo Procopio was absolutely right. What's done is done. The fire was nobody's fault. We can't spend the rest of our lives blaming ourselves—or each other—for what happened.

One of my favorite old movies used to be *It's a Wonderful Life*— that is before every local and cable TV station in the country began running it ten times a day around Christmas. Still, I'm always a sucker for the ending when George Bailey is surrounded by all his friends and neighbors who come to his rescue in a time of need. George learns that "no man is poor who has friends."

Throughout that initial week, and for weeks to come, Charlotte and I were constantly reminded of the blessing of friends in both small and grand ways. We didn't have to beg anyone for assistance. They flocked to Pacific Street on their own.

For instance, Larry Martinez and Cathy Boggs made the ninety-minute drive from Santa Barbara when they heard about the fire and volunteered to go through our closets, bundling up clothes to be taken to the cleaners. Karen Gray, a deputy district attorney, took the day off from work and attached herself to me. I couldn't sneeze without her approval. She drove around town and found us a storage unit that would take fire-damaged furniture. Without asking, Maggie Cox arranged for a dumpster to magically appear. Bill Roalman, then a city council member, improvised a wooden walkway across the gaping hole in the floor so we could access the rear bedrooms. Neighbors Courtney and Pete came over, ready to help in any way possible. The days and weeks to come would be filled with many acts of spontaneous and genuine kindness.

That first day after the fire, people continued to arrive at our front door, a solemn pilgrimage of the heart. Overcome with disbelief, they came in search of us. With each new person appearing at the front door, the tears swelled up again.

Somehow I began the week with this John Wayne macho idea that I was going to do all this myself. "*I don't need anyone's help. I don't want anyone's help,*" I told myself. Fortunately, that Neanderthal attitude evaporated quickly. Another lesson from Pet Grief 101: You're not the only one hurting. Others hurt, too. Especially other animal lovers. The thought of losing all their animal companions at once was overwhelming for people.

Their sentiments became a chant: "I own three dogs," or "I own four cats…. I can't imagine losing them all at once…. I can't imagine what you must be going through. I feel so terrible about what happened."

People needed some outlet for their own anguish and fears. During that first week especially, I spent as much time comforting others as I was being comforted. Despite my own trauma, I had to learn to be strong for others. Charlotte and I quickly realized that we weren't the only ones in pain.

We also had to learn to let others help in whatever way they could. An account was quickly set up at a local bank. Donations poured in. Good friends and total strangers started slipping money in my pocket—$10, $20, $100. I'd protest, but it was always pointless. "Take it," they'd insist. "You'll need it." And they were right. Others dropped off food and clothing. We learned not to argue. Just say thank you. We could never say it enough.

About fifty percent of our furniture and belongings were salvageable. The blue wing-back chair from the living room went in the trash. Too painful. Triptych, Tripper and Trio always slept there. Same thing for the couch. It survived the fire, but there was no way I could ever look at it again. When I saw the couch, I saw the five pets.

We threw away the animal food and water bowls, along with any rawhide bones or toys we stumbled across. I collected the dog leashes. The five collars and name tags would be returned to us later. Those we hung on to, now tucked away in a closet. We still can't bring them out because of the lingering pain. Still, it's important to maintain that connection, to have some memories. They come in all shapes and sizes.

I called Dr. Knighton that Monday afternoon. He offered us the opportunity to drive out and say one final farewell, but we declined. Sunday night was difficult enough without having to replay it. We had already said our good-byes. There was nothing more to add; our grief would only be rekindled. Woods Humane Society, a local nonprofit animal shelter, called to offer cremation for all five at no cost. After a brief discussion, we decided to accept the offer.

On this first day, shock had given way to disbelief. *This wasn't the way it was supposed to be. This isn't how we had imagined the end. Not all five going together. So sudden. No, not like this.* Tess was barely six months old. Trio was little more than eighteen months and even old Triptych probably had another four or five good years left. The property destruction was secondary, but I couldn't shake the knot in my stomach as I struggled to accept our loss.

Meanwhile, Charlotte had the film developed with the final photos of the animals that she had taken the day before they died. The photo quality isn't the best, but it remains impossible for me to erase those murky images from my mind. Smiling Tess next to a somber Topper on the couch. Tripper, Trio, and Triptych hovering innocently above them. And that's pretty much where they were sitting when we left that Sunday night for the party.

I remain haunted by those photos. It's difficult to even glance at them without cringing. Part of me—hell, all of me—just wants to reach into that photograph and grab each animal, pulling them all to safety; to scream and shout and warn them to run like hell for the front door. I try, but it doesn't work. They just stay on that couch, innocently staring off in five different directions. And all I can do is look away.

The *San Luis Obispo County Telegram-Tribune* ran an extensive front page story, complete with Topper's photo, on the following Tuesday morning. Within the article, the city's fire investigator, John Madden, attributed the cause of the fire to "a throw rug that was kicked on to the floor heater by one of the pets."

A throw rug from Sears. As soon as the firefighters explained it, we understood. There were hardwood floors throughout the house. A large area rug dominated our living room. There was a matching carpet runner in the back hallway and a third, smaller rug covered the wood floor just as people stepped out of the archway from the dining room.

The cats were always chasing each other around the house. That small piece of carpeting inevitably got shoved aside in any pursuit. This time it got shoved too far. Somehow the throw rug landed smack across the floor heater behind the couch. Maybe it was the cats. Maybe it was Tess—she liked to play, too. We'll never know. Does it really matter?

As the newspaper article reported, death was from carbon monoxide intoxication. Translation: Topper, Triptych, Tripper, Trio, and Tess fell asleep. There was no pain. No suffering. No trauma. They merely put their heads down and went to sleep.

Charlotte and I cling to that fact. Over and over, both of us have reminded ourselves and each other, "They merely put their heads down and went to sleep."

The firefighters told us the fire probably broke out shortly after our departure. The five pets had been dead for a long time. We were extremely lucky in one sense. Another twenty minutes, the firefighters warned, the whole house would have been engulfed in flames. Had our beloved animals actually burned to death, well, that would have felt unbearable.

I often find myself comparing notes with Charlotte about what happened exactly. And when. For some reason, I can never remember that I brought Triptych out of the house. Charlotte always has to remind me which cat I carried out; which cat she carried out. People have said my memory is clouded because of the twin wallop of grief and stress I still feel.

The radio station office manager, Vanessa Hollinger, called Bob and Janna's house with regular updates. She told us she was being swamped with messages, gifts and offers of temporary housing. Vanessa's constant reports aroused our curiosity. What were people sending to the radio station? What was there waiting for us? Though reluctant to go out in public, I finally drove to KVEC on Tuesday night to investigate.

There was a smattering of cards and letters on my desk, perhaps six or seven at most. I was surprised and confused since Vanessa kept referring to an "avalanche of mail." It wasn't until Wednesday that we discovered the truth. To guard the mail, especially any envelopes that might contain cash, Vanessa had wisely hidden everything in a box under her desk. There were dozens of letters, both mailed and hand-delivered, addressed to us. A similar pile of mail waited at the newspaper office. The outpouring would continue steadily for the next two months.

That Tuesday night at the radio station, something else left me speechless. Back in 1992, Topper and I had appeared in a series of newspaper ads for my optometrist, Dr. Jeff Blue. Topper and I posed side-by-side, laying on the floor together, with me wearing some fancy European-styled glasses. We were just doing Jeff a favor, however, the ad campaign was a success. Jeff had one of the black-and-white photos blown up and framed on display in his office.

Waiting for me at the radio station was that same large framed photograph. Jeff had brought it by after the fire, wanting me to have it. My eyes welled up as I clutched the frame. I felt so overwhelmed by his kindness.

The next morning, I made a point of stopping by Jeff's office. I swept through his waiting room like a blur and found him in the hallway. Wrapping my arms around him, I began sobbing. He was probably suffocating because I kept squeezing the poor guy so tightly.

"Thank you, thank you, thank you," I kept repeating through the tears.

"I didn't know if I should wait," Jeff replied. "A friend of mine just lost her husband. I called her up and asked if I should wait to give you the photo. She said not to wait. Don't ever wait. So I didn't."

"She's right," I said, crying even more. "You did the right thing. Don't ever wait. Believe me, you did the right thing. Don't ever wait."

With the help of friends, everything was moved out of Pacific Street by Wednesday afternoon. That's the last time I went inside that house. Pulling the front door closed, I swore that we would never return. What we were able to salvage went to the storage unit. The furniture could wait. Time to put the focus back on our deceased pets.

The cards, phone calls, and donations continued throughout the week, forcing us to accept the caring and mourning in the community. With each passing hour, it became clearer that this was more than simply our loss. On Wednesday, Charlotte and I talked, and I urged her to agree to a public memorial service. The heartfelt tribute to Congressman Walter Capps after his unexpected death lingered in my mind. I had seen the power of people coming together in grief. Perhaps some type of similar tribute to our animals would provide initial closure.

The unpredictable December weather ruled out any kind of outdoor ceremony. Not belonging to any particular church also limited our options. However, I knew immediately where the ceremony should take place. In May 1997, Charlotte had treated me to a special birthday gift. The Palm Theatre in San Luis Obispo is a wonderful, three-screen movie theater that specializes in alternative/art films. Theatre owner Jim Dee is a good friend who appears on my radio show every Friday morning to talk about movies. For my 44th birthday, Jim let us have his 150-seat main theater for a private showing of my all-time favorite movie, Casablanca. More than one hundred people showed up for the birthday screening. I've never had a more enjoyable birthday.

The best of times, the worst of times. So be it. We would return to the Palm Theatre for the memorial service. Jim offered the entire theatre without hesitation. The ceremony would take place in three days, on Saturday morning. Some people were bound to think us crazy for bothering with such a ceremony, but Charlotte and I plunged ahead with planning, not taking the time to worry. Another lesson from Pet Grief 101: Go with your heart, not the opinions of others.

We called our ceremony, "The Day that Love Is Spelled with a T."

San Luis Obispo County Telegram-Tribune   *November 16, 1995*

Cat & Dog

You can lead a horse to water, but you can't make him drink. I would also submit that you can put a collar on a cat, but you can't make him bark.

His name is Tripper. He's white with black splotches running down both sides, a miniature, pudgy cow-cat who meows and meows, constantly demanding more attention than Ross Perot.

He's my cat, I guess. After all, it was my idea. I'm the one who insisted to Charlotte that we brave the heavy rain last January to see this kitten at the Atascadero shelter. With Topper being so sick, friends had expected us to start looking for a new dog. No, I explained emphatically, no more dogs. Not now.

Yet something drove me to Atascadero that morning. Maybe I was trying to be a better husband, and let Charlotte get that second cat she's always wanted. Maybe I was concerned about our other cat Triptych being alone in the house. Or maybe, just maybe, this was about my own inability to cope with the pending loss of a pet.

One window closes, another opens. We brought Tripper home in the rain to Los Osos.

The sight of a second cat in the house should have been enough to make poor Topper just keel over in shock. He didn't. And he hasn't, so here it is November, and we still have three pets, instead of two.

Only one can bark. I think that's the problem. Going the twenty miles from Los Osos to Atascadero is a lot easier than going from a dog to a cat.

* * *

I come home, pulling into the garage. There are never any surprises when I open the door. Topper always bounces out, his tail wagging furiously. His excitement is obvious: *Hey Dave, great to see you! Where you been? What'd you bring me? I missed you! I really did!* I could be gone five minutes and still get this greeting.

Then Topper personally escorts me upstairs, his tail still wagging in perfect drum major precision. Tripper, meanwhile, lies stretched out along the window sill. After a few minutes, the cat finally looks over at me: *Oh, it's you. You're home.*

I walk out to get the mail. As I come back, I notice Tripper, back in the front window. I call up to him, excitedly waving my arms, trying to get his attention. He stares at the birds. Looks over at the barking dogs in the next yard. Takes in the whole universe of Los Osos, but never once looks down at me. I keep calling up, the cat keeps ignoring. Finally, I give up.

I lie down on the floor next to Topper. Sometimes I scratch his back and stomach. Other times, I just drape my arm over his side, and talk to him. The dog doesn't move.

Tripper strictly enforces a fifteen-second rule. I'm permitted to hold him, even welcome to scratch his stomach, but only for fifteen seconds. After that, he instinctively breaks away. *That's enough, pal,* he tells me.

We battle daily over the computer. Tripper seems to think it's his mother, because he's always lying across the monitor. I pull him off. He jumps back on. Back and forth, all day long.

"Stay off the computer. Off!"

I yell at Tripper, threatening him with cat reform school. It doesn't matter. Ten minutes later, Tripper's nestled again on top of you-know-where.

The only time I seem worthy of Tripper's attention is when he's hungry, which actually is much of the day, or at least that part when he's not sleeping. Tripper leaps up on the kitchen counter, suddenly becoming Pavarotti, his voice filling the house as he passionately demands his dinner.

An old, tired dog. A young hyperkinetic cat. Two different animals. Two different worlds.

* * *

Topper was back in surgery last month; more cancerous tissue was removed from his mouth. The next week he became quite sick, throwing up constantly, barely able to walk. We made one late-night run to the ever-patient Dr. Knighton for a shot and something to settle Topper's stomach.

The last few months have been good ones with my dog, but the surgery and the sickness bring everything back. The crying spells have started up again. I can't seem to stop.

Young Tripper caught me the other night, as I sat on the couch with Topper lying next to me. The cat leaped up on the coffee table, walked across my leg and settled on my lap. He purred loudly, still not looking at me, still not acknowledging me.

Tripper spent slightly more than his obligatory fifteen seconds, sniffed over at Topper, and then disappeared, no doubt looking for the computer. But even through the tears, I understood the message. And I knew then why we had driven to Atascadero in the rain last January.

Everything is going to be OK. In time. The collar is being passed to a new family pet. Perhaps Tripper can't bark for joy, but there's something to be said for living in a house that rings with Pavarotti.

FIVE

Every Seat Was Taken

I have always found a certain level of comfort at the veterinarian's office. Of course, that's easy for humans to say. We're not the ones being examined. No one is going to prick us with a needle or take a sample. Heck, we have it easy. We're just the escort. At most, the only pain and discomfort we suffer is likely to be when we're handed the bill.

Over the years, I've associated our routine visits to Dr. Knighton with the power of healing. If something appeared wrong with one of our animals—this dependable veterinarian would make it well. Tess needs a shot. Fine. Topper could use a teeth cleaning. No problem. Trio's stitches need to come out. Consider it done. The pets go in. They come out. Routine work, professionally done. Dr. Knighton always made them better.

Until that first Thursday after the fire. Then there was a completely different reason to drive out to Los Osos to see Dr. Knighton. It was time to bring our animals home. They were ready—but this time they would not be better.

I volunteered to make the twenty-minute drive from San Luis Obispo to rural Los Osos, sensing that this was not a task that Charlotte would relish. Throughout the week, I had been trying to shelter her as much as possible. Friends volunteered to ride along, but I shook them all off. I owed this to Topper, Triptych, Tripper, Trio, and Tess. All week I had been fighting back enormous guilt for what had happened, feeling trapped in that painful "if-only" nonsense. *I wasn't there for them Sunday night, but I'd be there for them today. This time, no harm would come to them.*

Late Thursday afternoon, I sped along the two-lane highway that cuts through the misty emerald-green Los Osos Valley, toward the Pacific Ocean. Repeatedly, I talked to myself, pretending to talk to our pets, but actually preparing myself for what waited at the end of the road. *I'm coming, gang. Hang on. I'm coming for you.*

When I arrived at the Los Osos Pet Hospital, the office manager stood waiting for me. She ushered me directly into one of the small, sterile examination rooms. How many times had I been there before? How odd it felt to be waiting there alone, without one of the pets along. There would be no healing this time, I reminded myself. Everything about this visit felt so different, so quiet.

I tried to brace myself for The Moment. Ever since Monday, I tried to prepare myself. But for what? All I could do was try to remain calm. *Take a breath. Then take another. Quickly.*

After what seemed an unsettling eternity, the door finally opened and the office manager slipped in, carrying a nondescript cardboard box with a brown paper bag jutting out of the top. She placed the box carefully on the examination table.

"Stay here as long as you want," she said softly, trying her best to comfort us. "Nobody will disturb you. We don't need the room." Then she made a graceful exit. I was too focused on the box to notice.

Deep breath, now another.

Slowly, I opened up the brown paper bag, but the jingling inside tipped me off to the contents. Five brightly colored pet collars. Five sets of faded and smudged pet tags. I put the crumpled bag aside, just barely beating the first wave of tears. Sunday night exploded again in my mind, one intense flashback after another. The tags and collars quickly went back in the bag. Out of sight. The memories wouldn't go away as easily.

Again, I reminded myself. *Deep breath...keep breathing.*

Wiping away the tears with the back of my bandaged hand, I began removing the five cedar boxes slowly from the cardboard box. The identification sticker was on the bottom of each box; I had to hold the boxes up high to read the labels.

The cats came first; Tripper, Trio, Triptych. Seeing their names printed on the labels only fueled my despair. The little cedar boxes were no longer anonymous. They were so lightweight, so small, further underscoring the innocence of our three cats, how they had no chance once the fire started.

I cradled each one in my arms for a moment, forgetting completely that they were cedar boxes. Talking to the three cats, I apologized again. I tried to reassure them. Or maybe I was trying to reassure myself. The casual observer would never had understood this scene, making me grateful to be alone.

Then came the two dogs. Their boxes were larger and heavier. More tears streamed down my cheeks as I lifted up one of the boxes. Tess. *Oh, dear, poor, young Tess.* This was all that was left of our little four-legged holiday epiphany. I couldn't bring myself to look at the final cedar chest because I knew who it was. For a moment I became angry. Topper and I had been through so much together over the last fourteen years. And that fire robbed me of the chance to say goodbye to my loyal animal companion, to bring his life full circle as Charlotte and I had planned.

How could this be? How could this be happening? We had five wonderful pets who were lively, playful, and spirited—they were the best. Four days later and this is all we have left of them. Five small, nondescript cedar coffins.

No amount of deep breathing could help. I gave up trying. Laying the boxes out side-by-side on the steel examination table, I recalled how all five had been with Dr. Knighton on this same table at one time or another. My hands started rubbing the boxes as if I were petting the animals, some type of spiritual transition in which I needed to accept what happened Sunday night.

Little snippets from their lives, our lives together, replayed in my mind like an old grainy movie. Topper and Tess on the beach together in Santa Barbara; Charlotte holding Triptych lovingly as he put his left paw on her shoulder; Trio staring down at me from atop a pile of Charlotte's sweaters in her bedroom closet; Tripper insisting on jumping up on top of my personal computer (again) as I tried to meet a deadline; Topper as a puppy in Indiana; Trio as a Christmas kitten; Tripper and Triptych curled up next to each other on the bed; Tess joyfully wagging the tiny stub of her tail every time I walked through the front door.

These vivid memories played out in stark contrast to the solitude and emptiness of the examination room. Between the sniffles, I tried to offer praise and reassurance, talking to the cedar boxes as if they were still our energetic gang, anxiously glued to my every word.

"I've come to take you home, guys," I said, not giving a damn about who might overhear me. "Charlotte and I are never going to leave you again. You'll always be with us, OK? Always. I swear."

For a long time I lingered in the examination room, trying to compose myself. I waited until I thought that Topper and Triptych and Tripper and Trio and Tess understood. Then, when I finally felt strong enough to be seen in public again and to trust myself behind the wheel, I lovingly packed up my friends and their belongings. The best I could offer to the grim-faced staff behind the counter was a mumbled "Thanks" as I scurried through the waiting room.

I drove ever-so-carefully back to San Luis Obispo, talking constantly throughout the drive to the brown cardboard box in the empty seat next to me. A somber, but anxious Charlotte greeted me at the front door as Bob and Janna struggled to set up their towering Douglas Fir tree in the living room. Two of Bob's grown daughters were home for the holidays and the family planned to decorate the tree after dinner. Charlotte had been swamped all day, juggling offers of free temporary housing, and keeping track of all the donations pouring in.

Standing in the doorway, holding that cardboard box, I felt like the classic grinch invading someone's holiday. We couldn't rush to the guest bedroom quick enough. One by one, the cedar boxes came out and Charlotte placed them gingerly on a nearby bookshelf. They needed to be out in the open. With us. Just like before.

"We're together again," my wife declared, taking a deep breath.

I pulled her close. "And we always will be," I whispered.

On Saturday morning, the day of the memorial service, Charlotte and I dressed simply. We arrived early at the theatre and immediately went to the small rear theatre. Waiting with some last-minute anxiety, we greeted a smattering of friends, not quite sure what to expect. Why were we doing this? Why would anyone care? Would anyone show up for a ceremony remembering three dead cats and two dead dogs on the Saturday before Christmas?

As people began arriving, they were given the opportunity to sign a memory book, offering them a chance to unload their own grief as well as help create a permanent record of the event. Various enlarged photos of Topper, Triptych, Tripper, Trio, and Tess greeted guests in the lobby.

Bill Roalman lightly strummed classical music on his guitar at the front of the theatre as people arrived. On the stage, the five cedar boxes were arranged, each draped with a single red rose and a name card. In the right front corner, propped up on an easel, rested the photograph of Topper and me from the optometrist's office.

The atmosphere was subdued, simple, and tasteful. We didn't want people to think we were *too* crazy.

Charlotte entered the main theatre early, wanting to sit in the second row with Eileen and Jim Robinson and their three young sons, J.B., Chris and John. The Robinsons had quite a four-legged menagerie themselves. Charlotte and I had never been overly fond of children, but the three Robinson boys were a delightful exception. Having grown very close to Charlotte, they would be her support system that morning.

The start of the ceremony grew near. The musicians continued to tune their guitars in the side hallway. Still feeling uncertain and more than a little confused, I stepped through the back entrance into the main theatre just before ten o'clock. I couldn't believe my eyes. Every single seat was taken.

Still more people crowded along the back and side walls. People continued to file in. Close to two hundred people were in attendance, including the mayor and two city council members. Many in the audience were familiar faces, others were complete strangers.

Then, just as the ceremony was about to begin, tall, lanky state senator Jack O'Connell strode in. At his side was Lois Capps, the widow of Congressman Capps. I was stunned by her unexpected appearance. Everything in our ceremony had been inspired by the tribute to her late husband, which Charlotte and I had attended the month before. Her warm embrace and encouraging smile erased any hesitancy I felt about the morning. If Mrs. Capps could smile after what she'd just been through, I knew things would be OK.

Music opened the service. In addition to Bill's guitar playing at the beginning, I also recruited a few local musicians to perform throughout the ceremony, each offering individual musical tributes interspersed throughout the hour. "Go with your heart," I urged, trusting their musical sensibilities. We were not disappointed.

I squeezed between Charlotte and young Chris Robinson. Chris's younger brother John stayed perched on Charlotte's lap for the entire hour, a human life preserver.

Jim Dee made the official welcome and offered a moment of silence so that we could all remember those special pets from our lives who were no longer with us.

Next, Ann Calhoun rose to read a poem by Thomas Carper entitled "A Guardian Tanya." Ann, who owns more basenjis than you can shake a biscuit at, called into my radio show that first Monday morning and read Carper's poem, prompting a strong response from our listeners. I asked Ann to read the poem again at the ceremony.

> Sensing when I must travel, she refuses
> To sleep downstairs. She comes into the bedroom.
> Nuzzles her biscuit into a corner,
> Circles twice and lies down at my feet.
> Her sleep is sound, and I sleep soundly too,
> As if we were two sculptures in an abbey
> Memorialized by a forgotten artist
> Who understood necessities of friendship.
> It's likely she will die before I die,
> And though I have no faith in streets of gold,
> I have half-confidence that I will meet her
> On this side of a bridge across death's river,
> Letting arriving spirits pat and scratch her,
> Or stretching out, her head between her paws
> As if for sleep, but with her eyes wide open,
> Watching, waiting, sure that I will get there,
> Sure that I will find her among thousands,
> Coming gladly with a leash to link us
> So we can go to death as on a walk.

Charlotte and I loved our pets equally, and we felt it was important that all five of our animals share the spotlight in this ceremony. For these tributes, we invited five friends who had some connection to our pets to speak.

Some were obvious choices. Don Ryujin, a Cal Poly psychology professor, and I had both taught together at DePauw University in Greencastle, Indiana. Don knew Topper when he was just a puppy. He knew the history and he understood the impact of Topper's death.

Janna Nichols, Charlotte's closest friend, had done so much for us during that critical first week. Janna would have the difficult challenge of speaking for our three-legged Triptych.

Wendy Martine was on duty at the North County Humane Society shelter that December afternoon in 1996 when I came wandering in with that "new-cat-on-my-mind" stare. She spent a patient thirty minutes with me, tolerating every inane question and second-guessing on my part. Then in the kitten room, the black-and-white tuxedo feline leapt off the upper shelf into my heart. She was the third cat in our lives, this young Trio. Wendy would speak for her.

Another close friend, novelist Catherine Ryan Hyde, would find the words to remember Tess. Topper and Tess had stayed overnight with Catherine at her Cambria home a week before the fire. Catherine was one of the few people who was actually able to say she knew Tess, making her the logical choice.

Finally, the most difficult challenge was finding someone for Tripper, our cat with an attitude. Tripper didn't like anyone or anything—most of the time—making him a most unlikely candidate for any type of sincere memorial. He needed someone special. I tapped my friend and former comedian Dave Hungerford. He was reluctant, wondering if he could be serious. "I don't want you to be serious," I replied. "I want you to be you. Tell jokes. Be yourself. Don't be afraid to push the envelope."

Dave didn't. He scored big, commenting on how people often try to humanize their pets. "Look at me. My cats are named Geoffrey and Stuart," Dave cracked. "If you think that's odd, you should talk to my oldest son, Fluffy." His mixture of jokes and sincere tribute even had Lois Capps smiling. Dave reminded all of us that both laughter and tears have a place at a memorial service.

Each of the five speakers connected with the audience in his or her own way. Charlotte and I were very grateful and touched by their loving words. Their tributes confirmed that our animals were special to people other than ourselves.

There is an old Quaker tradition at public meetings and weddings where time is reserved for comments from the floor. We decided to incorporate that into our memorial service toward the end of the hour. Even though I wanted to keep my direct involvement in the ceremony to a minimum, I did speak briefly at the beginning of the comment period.

After thanking the audience for supporting the idea of a pet memorial, I acknowledged Dr. Knighton and his staff who were gracious enough to join us that morning. And also a doleful Landlord Bill and his family, their hearts certainly broken almost as much as ours.

Then I had a confession to make. There had been a lot of soul searching on my part all week. Charlotte and I had never been closer than during these last six days, but that intense intimacy had made me realize something about our relationship.

"There can be a problem when you let too many animals in your house," I began. "Especially when you're married. It's too easy to let the pets substitute for you as a spouse. 'Oh, I don't have to worry about expressing love for my wife because she has Triptych.' Or 'I don't have to worry about trying to display affection because Tess and Topper are around. They're better at that than me. Charlotte has the pets. I can slide a little as a husband.'

"That's a mistake I've made too often," I admitted. "Animals are usually better at showing their emotions than humans, especially husbands. So I need to say today, before all of my friends, that I realize today how I have to be a better husband to Charlotte. To make up for the love that we have lost. I intend to be. And I'm only sorry that it took the loss of Topper, Triptych, Tripper, Trio, and Tess to make me realize this."

With that, I stopped. I didn't want to start crying. Our amiable friend, Dieter Nicklesberg, owner of two beautiful golden retrievers, jumped to his feet to begin the audience participation. He offered a rambling story about recently being at Laguna Lake during the noon hour with his two dogs. Dieter liked to throw a ball in the water for Maggie to fetch.

But something happened during one retrieval attempt. Maggie started struggling in the water. In front of several on-lookers, Dieter immediately stripped down to his underwear and dove into the lake, determined to rescue his dog. There was only one problem, Dieter explained, the lake was only about two feet deep. Maggie was fine. Dieter ended up more than a little red-faced, and soaked, standing in front of amused on-lookers in his dripping-wet underwear at high noon.

The audience roared, completely breaking the somber mood of the memorial, providing still another turn on the emotional roller coaster. Jim Dee would later report that after the memorial service, the floor of the theatre was a sea of crumpled tissues.

Charlotte and I stayed on at the Palm for almost a full hour after the ceremony. The receiving line was a long mixture of bereaved friends and complete strangers. Once again, we had to put aside our own grief to help all these wonderful people express their sadness.

Later in the day, while we gathered with friends for a private luncheon in Shell Beach, Charlotte pulled me aside and thanked me for organizing the memorial service. "It helped me a lot," she said. "The ceremony was wonderful, all of it."

TRIBUTE TO TESS

If it helps at all to know this, Tess, I was the youngest in my family, too. I know how easy it is to get lost in those big shadows cast by your big brothers and sisters. And people say, "I know who you are. You're Topper's little sister." And you are. But you're also Tess. A fine puppy in your own right who can stand on your own four feet in or out of any big shadow. Even Topper's. So, a few words to make sure Tess doesn't get lost.

When I close my eyes and think about Tess, what I remember most is how light she was, and how light on her feet. She had a thin, lithe, light little body, with a high tuck and long, long legs. And she stood very high on the pads of her paws, like she was walking on her toes, or the balls of her feet. If she were here, and could talk, I'm sure she'd say, "The better to run and dance and be a puppy and just love the hell out of life."

And she had a narrow, delicate face. Rather feminine. And brilliant dark eyes. And, pound for pound, more ears than I've ever seen on a dog in my life. If she were here, she'd probably say, "The better to hear everything in the world that interests me." And of course what interested Tess was everything in the world.

I'm grateful that Tess died not in the pound but quietly in the home of her family, who loved her. Because in the pound nobody tells you what a good puppy you are. And she was a good puppy.

Less than two weeks ago I had the privilege of waking up in the morning with Topper and Tess in our house, my mother's and mine. I opened my eyes, and there was that face. Those ears. Those bright, dark eyes. She had her head stuck through the doggy door into my room. Just checking to see if I was awake.

And when she saw I was, that's all she needed to know. She came rocketing through that doggy door, and came tearing around the bed, and jumped, but just her front half landed on the bed. And with that little stubby tail going she kissed my face and told me that it was a miracle of great joy that I woke up. Is it any wonder that we love our pets so much?

That good morning kiss is what Tess gave me that nobody can take back. I'm sure that in the short time Tess lived with Dave and Charlotte she gave them many such kisses, many such moments. So much of what we love in this life isn't really ours to keep, but those moments are ours, and they can never be taken away.

So in closing, to my friends Charlotte and Dave: I love you both dearly, and my heart is so with you now. I'm sure I'll get it back eventually, but for now it's with you. And that's OK. You're welcome to it.

To my friend Topper: I'll miss you, because I knew you well, and for a long time.

And for my friend Tess: I'll miss you, because I knew you just well enough to know that I wanted to know you for a long time, and I wanted to know you well....

One more message for Tess, if you're listening: Good puppy, Tess.

– *Catherine Ryan Hyde*
Palm Theatre Memorial Service,
December 20, 1997

Tribute to Topper

I was very moved when Dave asked me to say a few words about Topper today. I know how much Topper means to both Dave and Charlotte, and I hope I can do justice to his memory. Yet, I know it is impossible to capture the specialness of Topper in words. You can't talk about him, you just need to meet him to know how special he is.

In trying to find what to say today, I naturally thought about all the wonderful times I could remember with Topper. I started at the beginning when Dave and I were young and we were back at DePauw University in Greencastle, Indiana. While Dave and I were idealistic professors boring students with our lectures, Topper, the young Topper, was fast becoming the big dog on campus, making every student he met smile and giggle as he happily greeted them. Topper was so full of life, so full of energy, and he so much liked to meet new people and invite them to play. It was fun just to be around the dog because he enjoyed living so much.

And it was obvious from the beginning that he was special. As Dave says, Topper was special before there was a newspaper column and before he was mentioned on the radio. Topper was always special to Dave and to Charlotte and to everyone who met him.

Despite the joys of remembering the early years, one of my most vivid memories came near the end. I remember a later time, a time in San Luis Obispo when Dave had become a popular radio talk show host and I had become a Cal Poly professor. Topper had been diagnosed with cancer and wasn't expected to live very long. I went on sabbatical leave to Maryland, expecting to find out that Topper had died when I returned.

To my delight and amazement, he was still alive and scratching when I got back. I visited Dave and Charlotte to see Topper. With all of Topper's aches and pains, he still slowly got up from the floor, and came over to greet me. He looked up at me with those warm eyes and his floppy ear and nodded as if to say, "Welcome back, my old friend!" He was no longer young, and he was very sick, but by his actions I was reminded again how very special he always was.

In between these memories there are so many, many more. But, in thinking about them, it struck me that all of them embody a sense of warmth and joy and life. Topper could always make us smile and laugh and feel free for the moment. For an instant he made our lives a little brighter, a little kinder and a little warmer. Just as importantly, for a moment Topper made us all better people. For a moment we were kinder, warmer, and more humane. For a moment we gave the best of ourselves. And now he is gone and he leaves us with fourteen years of grace and joy and kindness.

Topper, my old friend, we will all miss you.

– *Dr. Donald Ryujin*
Palm Theatre Memorial Service,
December 20, 1997

Six

There Is Only Now

*I*n the weeks following the fire, Charlotte and I heard from a wide variety of people, all offering support and condolences in amazingly different ways. One woman dropped off a memory quilt, complete with photos of our five animal companions who had died. An artist who chose to remain anonymous crafted beautiful ceramic bowls in honor of Topper and Triptych. And two local musicians were inspired to write "Topper the Teacher," a song complete with the refrain, "You were the greatest teacher, Topper. May your lessons never end. For just as long as we remember, you'll be our teacher and our friend."

Hundreds of personal messages poured in from across the county as well as nationally. We read every word, no matter how difficult, simply stunned by the demonstration of concern and encouragement. It was so gratifying to discover that we were not alone in our feelings and especially in our grief for our five departed animals. The following is a sampling of the comments we received.

"Hopefully no one will be foolish enough to say, 'You'll get over this in time.' Because we don't, really—not entirely—and I think that's as it should be. If a foreign object became lodged in our body and could not be moved, our body would have no choice but to heal around it.

"When a loss of this magnitude lodges in our heart, we rebuild ourselves around it and the scar becomes a significant part of who we go on to be. Maybe the best we can hope for is that it will break our heart in such a way to increase its capacity for later use. That is my wish for you."

"...I learned some valuable lessons from your pets. Topper embodied a fighting spirit and reminded me that while life holds no guarantees, if you live in the moment, life can be enriching and entertaining. Your cats taught me that everyone comes in different shapes, sizes and breeding. It isn't how you start your life, or end your life. It's about how you live your life.

"Animals bring out a depth of love within us that we may not have felt capable of expressing. I believe that is their gift to us. I hope that gift and the lessons that your pets have taught me can help you with the pain you feel."

"There are no easy words at times like these—no ways to understand that which seems so senseless. Your lives were increased by the quality of love and affection given and received from those you loved and lost. For however long, each of those animals chose you to be their human companions. You could ask for no greater gift than to remember that love.

"Death teaches us the harshest lesson. That there is no tomorrow, no later. There is only now."

"Sometimes it's so hard to understand the 'whys' of life. Unfortunately, sometimes we just never understand them.

"When my father died—Mom and Dad had been married to each other for more than fifty years—I asked Mom how she kept her heart content, kept a positive attitude, and stayed a happy person. She said to me, 'Every day when I first get up in the morning, I look in the mirror and thank God for all the wonderful times I had with Tom and I think about three wonderful times we had. Each day I think of a different three times. This helps me feel grateful, which in turn, helps me feel happy and content.'

"I hope Mom's wisdom helps you in the days ahead!"

"Today there is a hole in the heart of everyone who has ever loved a pet. As soon as we get them we are losing them. That's what makes it so hard to decide whether to go through it again. And that is why, when people learned of your loss, it cut so many of them so deeply.

"Is it foolish to love anything so much? The Bible says 'God is love,' and 'We love because He first loved us.' If God didn't want us to love dogs, why did He make them the way they are? And why does He continue to make so many of them? If we don't exercise our capacity to love, to care, how will we all end up?"

"Tragedies like this are never welcome, but the dark side of life is what truly tests us. Living in the light is easy and enjoyable. The dark side is what molds us as individual souls."

"I have no magic words to ease your pain, but as someone once told me, it takes a very special person to welcome a pet into their lives for we know the stay will be far too short. You both gave much to your animals and enhanced their time here by receiving all they had to give back. Love continues, and soon it will be through a smile and not a tear."

"I also have five pets. I've tried to prepare myself to lose the two older ones. Maddy's thirteen and blind, but still a great dog. Jack got his cancer back, but continues to defy the odds. My girls and boy are the stable part of my life, more so than my job, my home, even my sweetie. I just wanted you to know that ever since your loss, I appreciate them a little more each day. Thank you."

"My husband and I made a conscientious decision to not have children many years ago. When we separated several years later, our great Dane Sheeka came with me. When Sheeka died I felt a physical and emotional loss similar to the loss of my father. Three weeks later, I rescued sweet Goldie from the pound—never to replace Sheeka, but to share my life. Eleven years later, we share a bond I could never explain."

"It's been ten years since my mom put our family dog, Peppie, to sleep. She didn't tell me she was going to do so, and I never had the chance to say goodbye. Peppie was like a brother to me. I grew up with him; he was the sweetest dog in the world and such a good friend. It's been ten years and I've cried almost every day over the loss of my dog. I bear a greater pain that I will never be able to forgive myself for.

"The morning of the day my mom took him, I hit Peppie. I hit him because he was howling at the door for my mom and it was aggravating me. Do you know how bad I hate myself now? I sob every time I think about it and it's been ten years."

"When my yellow lab Murphy, my best friend, died, I thought my heart would never be the same. The hardest part I faced was not having the chance to say goodbye…. I guess I have learned that our pets will always stay in our hearts no matter what. If and when you get another pet, they will never take the place of a lost one, but they will bring joy and happiness in their own special way. The hardest part is trying not to compare them to the ones we have loved and lost."

"There is something about the way a pet stares at you like you are the center of its universe that calms the heart and mind like few other things. Pets choose to love us and we are honored by that. You must know that their spirits live on, as do ours."

"My fifteen-year-old dog and fifteen-year-old cat died last spring. I adopted a mother cat and two kittens within a few weeks from a local shelter. My vet told me, 'I always feel it is a tribute to past pets when someone takes a step to bring new ones into your life.' I have a feeling that before long you will build a new animal family. Those pets will be very lucky and much loved."

"My heart goes out to you in this very sad time. Topper, Triptych, Tripper, Trio, and Tess were a big part of your life. Please try to take each day as it comes. Cherish all the good and wonderful times you had with them. Don't try to hold in what you're feeling, talk to your friends, go ahead—scream, yell or cry. It does help.

"Each of your pets were very fortunate to have you as their owners. All of the love and care you gave them made their life a full and happy one. Think of your short time with them as a blessing and how wonderful it was that they were a part of your life. Remember—a pet is not forever, but its loving memory is."

"We know the heartbreak of pet loss. When those memories return, the thought that helps the most is that 'We were *privileged* to have had those pets—for however short or long that was!' This thought helps! And any new member to our special little family in the future will again be a privileged opportunity for us."

"We totally understand your devastation over your loss. We feel sorry for people who can't bond with pets and have that wonderful relationship. We don't think we could ever be without pets…. It surprised us that we found a new special dog, Murphy, only six weeks after losing Muffin, our dog of more than seventeen years. It hasn't diminished our love for her or our missing her, but Murphy has brought us such great joy! So we hope you too will find some new friends—they won't diminish, only enhance, your love for your lost friends."

"I called my daughter-in-law recently and she was so choked up that she could hardly speak. I asked what was wrong and she told me the news about your loss…. We lost our wonderful terrier last October from lung cancer. He was eight years old and we are still heartbroken. We did all we could to save him, but it just wasn't meant to be. We went three weeks without a dog and I just couldn't stand it, so we went and got a new ten-month old terrier. He'll never take our 'Mister's' place but we go on. So please hang in there."

"I've become a cat man lately, but I still love dogs. I sure thought Topper was a great dog. Fires are such horrible things, even when no one gets hurt. When I was a boy, our house burned down and it was a devastating experience. In the moment of silence during your memorial service, I remembered every animal I had ever befriended."

"My advice to you is to work your head off, get out, be involved and let time get about the job of healing (If you keep picking at a sore, it won't heal). One of life's great lessons gets learned; and you know you won't learn the hard stuff unless you are forced. Wisdom is earned."

"As a pet owner/parent, I can appreciate your sense of loss. In November 1996 I lost my little three-legged black bobtail cat Mocha (Spanish meaning one without a limb) due to kidney failure. Mocha and I were pals for more than sixteen years. I still miss her—she taught me a lot of lessons about enduring whatever life tosses your way, about growing old gracefully, and even how to let go. Still, the emptiness is there. Your grief over your loss is very real, no matter what anyone else may say."

"In time, I know there will be new pets for you. You're both needed too much. They're waiting at the shelter for you. I bet the cats and dogs have a lottery going to see who will be lucky enough to come home with you. Because that's what it will be like for them to be picked by you—it will feel like they've just won the lottery!"

San Luis Obispo County Telegram-Tribune   June 10, 1997

The Need To Feel Kneaded

I am not, by any stretch of the imagination, known for wearing exotic sleepwear. A simple pair of shorts has been my modus operandi since high school when I first rebelled against wearing pajamas.

So now I own a lot of shorts; and two bathrobes, both presents from Charlotte. No, I obviously don't sleep in my bathrobe, but it's one of the first things I reach for in the morning. They're the closest things to sleepwear that I own.

One is a white silk robe, a beautiful Christmas present from my wife. I have worn it exactly twice, but this is a family newspaper, so I can't provide the details.

It's very nice, but I'm not exactly a white silk kind of guy, so the robe waits quietly in my closet, like the lonely wife eager for her sailor to come home from the sea.

There's also the comfortable, red terry cloth robe, faded at the elbows, sleeves now too short, marked by more than a few toothpaste stains, long overdue to become a Goodwill ambassador, if you catch my drift.

But the red robe stays nearby, despite the stains and the worn material. It's not that I'm sentimental, mind you. I really have no choice. You see, we have a cat who seems to think this threadbare and frayed robe is actually his mother.

Tripper will be three in July, a paunchy white and black cat we adopted a few years back. We took him on faith, and he's actually turned out to be a great little family member. (Topper might argue, as far as cats go, that is.)

However, there's a noticeable difference between Tripper and our oldest cat, the three-legged Triptych. Triptych is a lover. Tripper is a loner. He doesn't like to be held. He doesn't even like to be touched. A simple, friendly scratch on the head is enough to start his tail snapping. Everything is on his terms. This is one macho Sylvester Stallone cat.

Except when he sees me in my old terry cloth bathrobe. Then, well, then, poor Tripper instantly becomes my best friend, clinging to me like one of those Garfield cats in the back window of a car.

One moment he's John Wayne at the Alamo; the next, he's little Bambi in the woods, crying for his mother.

"He's nursing," Charlotte, the family feline expert, always explains. "Poor Tripper must have been taken away from his mother too early. Your bathrobe is warm and soft. It reminds him of fur."

So Tripper is prone to pounce on my shoulders when he sees the bathrobe. He kneads at the material with both front paws, sucking and slobbering all over me. This little guy becomes an instant love machine, purring and purring with a level of content normally reserved for catnip. Tripper clings intensely until I physically detach myself.

Fine for him, but my schedule comes grinding to a complete halt. Ever try to work, or even read the newspaper, when there's an eight-pound cat attached to your right shoulder? When the bathrobe disappears, so does Tripper, faster than a one-night stand.

"Is he always going to be like this?" I ask Charlotte. "Isn't there anything we can do?"

My wife doesn't think so. I suppose I could shift over to that white silk number, or even just buy a new robe. Maybe later. Not right now. The old red terry cloth robe stays, toothpaste stains and all. Tripper was separated once from his mother—no reason to make him suffer again.

So here I sit. Another morning going to waste. A slobbering tub-of-a-cat on my shoulder, unable to get anything done. Still, Tripper's soft purring reaches through, even to a sour grinch like me. Because, as we all know but rarely confess, it's nice to feel kneaded.

SEVEN

The Elephant On The Coffee Table

*T*he second wave of grief for us began eight days after the fire. The critical first phase was over. Much had been accomplished. We were out of Pacific Street and our pets had been cremated. The wonderful Saturday morning memorial service had reminded Charlotte and me of how many great friends surrounded us and how many people were sharing our loss. Now it was time to try and move forward. Admittedly baby steps, but still go forward. Somehow.

That same morning, Charlotte and I moved into a new, albeit temporary house in San Luis Obispo. A colleague of Charlotte's from Cuesta College had recently married and moved in with her husband. The woman had lived in the same house for twenty-five years and, being sentimental, was reluctant to put it on the market. So there it sat, completely furnished, but empty of any life.

Located in the upscale Monterey Heights neighborhood, the A-framed house was spectacular. We had a sweeping panoramic view of the city from the living room appointed with expensive antiques. A master bedroom loft overlooked the main floor. My ophthalmologist lived three doors to the left and the primary sponsor of my radio show occupied the towering three-level complex directly across the street.

We were given the key and told to stay there as long as we needed. One month, two months, a year—it didn't matter. At every turn, someone in the community was there for us.

Despite such generosity, the transition remained difficult, awkward, and painful. Here we were in a house, not ours, with furniture that was not ours. Nothing was ours. Worst of all, there were no pets, only a constant, eerie quiet. We walked through the front door, only to be greeted by graveyard silence.

Our meager supply of sedatives was long gone. Crying spells continued as part of our daily routine since neither one of us felt any shame or reluctance about the tears. Charlotte and I continued to grow closer during this initial period. We understood the pain the other felt. A magazine survey on pet loss found that grief over pet loss is very common, but hundreds of people interviewed stated a belief that they felt they were the only ones ever to grieve over departed animal companions. We understood.

The strategy we adopted was to try and keep busy. Charlotte scribbled thank you notes and worked on finances. I sorted through photo albums, pulling out pictures that had been spared by the fire. Yet the effort was never enough. Everyone else eagerly prepared for the holidays while we remained zombies, merely going through the motions, living alone in a beautiful, empty house.

One morning I scanned through the local paper, not really looking for anything in particular. A letter to the editor caught my eye. Someone wrote a letter, taking Charlotte and me to task for not having a pet door on Pacific Street. Those five animals might still be alive today, the person argued.

Unbelievable. *Merry Christmas, Dave and Charlotte.* I tossed the newspaper aside in disgust. Here we were, in the early stages of our grief, being publicly attacked for supposedly not caring about our pets. The Monday morning quarterbacking had begun.

There was a working smoke detector in the house on Pacific Street, but no sprinkler system. The smoke detector was destroyed in the fire.

None of our neighbors reported hearing any alarm that Sunday night. Nor did we have a pet door because Triptych, Tripper and Trio were all declawed indoor cats. Charlotte never let them outside and I agreed with her decision. The cats would have been impossible to control with a pet door.

An escape to safety? Perhaps. Maybe. Possibly. Would any have escaped that night? Well, we could debate that question endlessly, but Charlotte and I chose not to. We believe we made the right decision then. Even with a new home and a new family of pets, we still don't have a pet door.

My parents were flying down from Seattle to spend Christmas with my older brother Bob. Charlotte and I had originally planned to drive to Los Angeles that Tuesday and join everyone for a big family celebration. However, we felt the need to scale down our visit. We would drive down Wednesday afternoon and stay until Friday. That would be plenty of time. My parents are both 82 years old. I wanted them to see me in person to prove we were OK. And, frankly, I guess I assumed that they, as family, would be a comfort to us.

Neither Charlotte nor I really wanted to make the trip. We certainly weren't in any mood to celebrate Christmas. It felt more comfortable in the womb-like safety of the temporary house, as opposed to being around others, especially strangers, or in crowds. There's something safe about being alone, seeming in control. But we felt obliged to go. We reassured one another, "Things will be OK— our family will understand."

On the way out of town, we stopped at the newspaper office to pick up yet another bundle of mail. Charlotte read assorted letters out loud as we zoomed south on Highway 101 for Los Angeles. Then she came across a thick manila packet. A well-meaning teacher at a local elementary school had shared the news of our fire with her fourth and fifth grade social studies classes. Her students decided to write letters to us with one rather curious twist. Many of the young students wrote to us pretending to be Topper, Triptych, Tripper, Trio, or Tess.

> Dear Dave and Charlotte,
> Hi, it's me, Tess. I just wanted to let you know that I'm doing just fine up here. When you get up here I'll probably be the first one to greet you. So don't worry so much about me….

> Dear Dave and Charlotte,
> It's me, Topper. I'm talking to you from heaven. I'm sorry you lost me in the fire. But I want you to know you'll always be the first person in my heart. I hope you have a Merry Christmas and a Happy New Year….

> Dear Dave and Charlotte,
> This is Topper. I'm doing fine. So is Tess, Trio, Triptych, and Tripper. We're in a good place. We love you and miss you a lot. Thanks for taking care of us once again. We love you!

Charlotte stopped after the third letter. This was too much. These students meant well, but this type of letter felt too intrusive and eerie with young students pretending to be our dead pets.

Arriving in Los Angeles that Christmas Eve afternoon, Charlotte and I realized just how big a mistake we were making. Having left our sanctuary in San Luis Obispo, we were now operating outside our newly established comfort zone. This was the world of non-pet owners. Nobody in our family had any real clue about the extent of our ordeal during the last ten days.

The minute we walked in the front door, Charlotte and I became the elephant on the coffee table. Coming home for the holidays, bringing our baggage with us.

From the very first day after the fire, I knew that not everyone understood. There were several calls to the radio station from people who couldn't grasp "the big deal over some dead animals." We also heard, second- and third-hand, about other perplexed people, wondering why Charlotte and I had needed to take extended time off from work.

The owner of the radio station, Frank Sheahan, could not have been more kind, more generous or more understanding in his support for Charlotte and me. He checked in on us almost daily, even when he was in Lake Tahoe for the holidays. Frank was one of the first people to show up at the memorial service.

On the other hand, Julia Aguilar, the then-publisher of the *Telegram-Tribune*, where I had written articles for the previous nine years, never bothered to send a note and never once called. It's not that she's a cruel person. Our loss, for whatever reason, simply wasn't an important issue for her.

So I was hoping, as we began the Christmas holiday with my family, that they would at least try to understand. Bob and his wife Anne are certainly good people, caring and supportive. However, they're not really pet people. Bob is allergic to cats, so in their almost thirty years together, my brother and sister-in-law have never had an animal in their house. They were always nice to Topper, but they didn't ever understand the bond between us. Bob and Anne acted sincerely concerned and upset at the news of our fire, but given the absence of animals in their lives, I don't think they had a true sense of the profound grief that Charlotte and I were experiencing.

Things started off on a hopeful note. We spent late Wednesday afternoon together, all sitting around in the family room—my elderly parents, Bob, Anne and my two twenty-something nephews Mark and Doug. They scanned the newspaper articles we had brought along. They peppered us with plenty of questions. They were glad to see us. But....

First came the mantra from Mom and Dad. Over and over again. "Move on, David. Get over it. What's done is done," my parents urged. They weren't trying to be rude or insensitive, but this was how my parents always dealt with bad news. Don't talk about it, just move on. They simply had no idea as to the true depth of our grief. Charlotte and I might as well have been talking to the wall.

The other immediately apparent fact was that Bob and Anne were not about to alter their holiday plans to accommodate our situation. They had Christmas Eve already mapped out. Off to church at 6 p.m. Then over to dinner with the family of their new daughter-in-law. We were certainly welcome to come along if we wanted, but the rest of the family saw no need to change their schedule to accommodate our grief. As much as I wanted to be with Mom and Dad, as much as I needed to try and connect with them, that moment, painfully, would have to wait.

The full extent of my family's insensitivity unfolded the next afternoon, Christmas Day. Joining us for Christmas dinner were several members of Anne's family, including her brother-in-law Jimmy, who has known us for years. Jimmy loved animals, so when he bounced into a house full of relatives Thursday afternoon and saw me, he unknowingly asked, "Hey, Dave, tell me, how's that great dog of yours? How's Topper?"

Charlotte and I exchanged stunned glances, both of us in total, jaw-dropping disbelief at the question. No member of my family had thought it necessary to inform their other guests about our enormous personal loss.

I couldn't keep the bitterness out of my response. "Well, Jimmy, actually, he's dead."

I love my brother and I know he wasn't trying to hurt us. As a non-pet owner, Bob simply hadn't thought things through, not aware of how all this was causing the entire holiday atmosphere to become tainted for us. Charlotte and I were the sorrowful intruders, spoiling the celebration for everyone else. We wanted to grieve. The family wanted to celebrate. Opposites were colliding.

Later on that night, my simmering frustration finally snapped. Poor Dad brought up the need for me to just "forget about it" once too often. In a firm but angry tone, in front of still more visiting friends, I suddenly turned on my 82-year-old father.

"I won't forget about it," I barked. "I am grieving. You have no idea of what I'm going through. Move on? I don't want to move on. I've lost just about everything in the world that I care about, Dad. You have to let me grieve for what I've lost." An awkward silence fell over the room.

Dad never mentioned the subject again. It was my turn to feel guilty for shrieking at my ailing father. This had become the Christmas from hell. I wanted to be anywhere else but in that house.

But Dad was right about one thing. It definitely was time to move on. So Charlotte and I bailed the next morning, racing home to San Luis Obispo. This time, we were actually relieved to find an empty house waiting for us.

Another important lesson from Pet Grief 101: Stay away from people who don't understand, even if it's family.

I didn't think this fragile family situation could get any worse. Then I had a conversation with my mom in Seattle a few weeks later. Clearly agitated, she expressed her disgust in overhearing still another adult family member tell "dogs on fire" jokes to his children, clearly referring to our loss.

Jokes about dead dogs? From a family member?

Overnight, the deepening cracks in our family took on seismic proportions. A small fracture now seemed more like the Grand Canyon.

Syndicated newspaper columnist Ellen Goodman once observed that human hearts "recover faster from surgery than from loss." She's absolutely right, but recovered, or not, we had to return to work at some point. Charlotte's colleagues at Cuesta College were supportive, but some seemed clearly puzzled. One particular co-worker surprised us by asking Charlotte whether we were grieving because of the loss of our home and so many possessions. Apparently, the loss of animals didn't register with her. Charlotte reported back to work in early January.

I returned to the radio show on January 7, my sixth anniversary broadcast. The two-hour program hardly offered a celebratory note as I spent most of the morning thanking the community and accepting supportive calls from listeners. It was a struggle to reach noon without completely losing my composure. I made it—barely.

The next morning posed even more of a challenge as I decided to spend the entire second half of the program on the issue of pet loss. Other topics would be easier to discuss, but none were more timely given what had happened. No matter how painful this might be, I had to seize the opportunity to educate others that grieving for pets is nothing to be ashamed about, and also to hear that I wasn't the only one with tears in my heart.

When the national news feed ended at 11:05, I skipped the usual musical opening and told my listeners a story.

"This is what I did last night," I began. "And it just kind of came over me. A few months ago, I wrote a newspaper column in the *Telegram-Tribune* about my cat Tripper. He was a black-and-white "cow cat"—white with these black splotches. Tripper was a cat with an attitude. He just didn't like people. He always set the terms of the relationship, but there was one exception—whenever I put on my old, red terry cloth bathrobe. If I did that, then Tripper, well, he'd suddenly become Mr. Nice Guy and he would not leave me alone. We had a very special relationship based on that bathrobe, and as crazy as it sounds, that's the way that it was."

My eyes stayed closed as I spoke. I didn't want to be distracted. Images of Tripper quickly filled my head. The others wouldn't be far behind.

"So we had the fire and we sent our clothes to the dry cleaners and most of the clothes were saved and they came back. I was going through things last night and I came across the red bathrobe. The bathrobe was saved and it looked fine, but there was no way I could ever wear that bathrobe again. So I folded it up and put it in the Goodwill box.

"Now, as you know, we had the five pets cremated and put in little cedar boxes. Right now, they're sitting in the living room of the temporary house where we're staying. It's not a shrine—we just have them there, near us. We want to stay close to them."

In six years and one day behind the microphone, I've never had a more difficult on-air moment. In a matter of seconds, the previous three weeks went flashing before my eyes, one horrible image after another. My voice cracked and my eyes welled up, but I pressed on.

"So last night, what I did is that I suddenly went over to the Goodwill box and I pulled out the bathrobe and I cut out with scissors a little piece of the bathrobe and I put it over Tripper's wooden box...." Tears streamed down my face and I had to pause for a few seconds to regain my composure. I wrapped up the story: "...because he was always on that bathrobe and I always want him to be."

Two guests joined me for the ensuing discussion. Ingrid Pires was the pet loss facilitator for Hospice of San Luis Obispo County. Ingrid had experienced both human and animal loss in her life and she worked with others as a counselor on a daily basis. Her perspective would be important. Sandy Rakestraw from the North County Humane Society also joined us because of her experience with animals and the pet loss she had encountered in her own life.

As we began talking, Ingrid pointed to my bathrobe story and my attempt to explain the connection between my relationship with Tripper and his relationship with the bathrobe.

"For those of us who do love animals, no explanation is needed," Ingrid said. "For the rest, it's important to realize that animals fill a unique niche in our lives, but it's not so different from the ones that people fill." Ingrid offered the example of an orphaned child to show how emotional bonds can be formed.

"If we bring home a child through the adoptive process, we don't have a biological relationship with that child, but we come to love that child just the same. If that child happens to be mute, then we can't get words back from that child, but we love that child just the same. If that child is deaf, we can't give words to it, but we love that child just the same. And if that child looks up at us with eyes of love, we know that that child loves us back. So we don't need words. We don't need biological ties. We don't even have to be in the same species to have the love be there. And if the love is there, when we lose that love, we grieve."

Ingrid explained how pets can be the main source of unconditional love for many people, if not the only source. "The depth of the grief is related to how much of our day we spend with them, how much history we have together, how important they've been throughout our lives. Pets play a unique role in loving us."

Sandy agreed that no matter how many pets we have in the course of our lives, we never get used to the grieving process. For her, it's an inherent part of adopting a pet. "If you have children, your children are supposed to outlive you," Sandy suggested. "But with a pet, you can technically have generation after generation of pets because their lives are shorter and so we have to do a lot of telling good-byes in our lifetimes to our pets. It's no less painful because it is an animal."

She felt that most people who don't understand pet loss typically don't have pets of their own, or they may have pets who are secondary to other family members. "But when the pet is your best friend, when you see it in the morning when you get out of bed, when you come home at night and it's the first thing that greets you at the door, it's very much like a family member."

Ingrid and Sandy were sounding great, very articulate and supportive as they reinforced each other's comments. The atmosphere inside the booth could not have been more positive. I began talking about what happened with my family over Christmas and how surprised Charlotte and I had been.

Ingrid responded initially by stressing the need for people to accommodate those in grief. If it's impossible, she said, people who are grieving need to alter their routine. She mentioned one family who had experienced a loss during a Christmas holiday. For the next four years, they went to the Bahamas in December, rather than be at home with the memories.

According to Ingrid, there are four major tasks to grieving. She doesn't like the word "stages" because grief doesn't come in a nice orderly fashion.

"The first is accepting the reality of the loss," Ingrid said. "We're not ready to accept the reality of the loss right up front. Yes, we know, our intellect knows these loved ones have died, but we're not ready to feel the fullness of it right away. So we do this gradually over time. The second task is experiencing the pain and indeed all of the emotions. Again, this comes over time and we need to recognize that denial is not a four-letter word. Denial is a wonderful thing that lets us do it at our pace. Because the paradox of grief is that we all experience it, but we all do it differently."

Everything Ingrid said clicked with me. Normally, I would have gone to a commercial break by then, but I didn't want to stop the conversation. "The third task," Ingrid continued, "is adjusting to the environment without that loved one or ones. When you wake up without five little ghosts dogging your steps. And the fourth—and when you've got this one socked away, you know you're pretty well over the worst of it—you can reinvest in other relationships."

Sandy stressed that there's really no timetable to recover from grief. It's very personal, and there's no instruction book. "You have to make it up as you go along. And Dave, you were explaining about cutting out the piece of bathrobe and putting it on the urn. I think that's important because since there are no guidelines, I think it's important to do what you feel like doing. And if you hadn't done that—I mean you might think you're crazy when you're doing it. But if you don't do it, you might think, 'Well, why didn't I do it? Because someone might laugh or scoff?'"

I finally stopped for a commercial break, and off-air, I repeatedly thanked both Sandy and Ingrid for participating, and being so open in their remarks. This was not an easy subject for anyone to discuss, but I was sure that the listeners weren't deserting us for Rush Limbaugh. When the next segment began, I asked Ingrid what people going through pet loss might say to colleagues or bosses to help them understand.

"I always ask them to look around in their lives for who they love the most, who they are deeply attached to and how they would feel if that person suddenly died," responded Ingrid.

Sandy called it "a process," a matter of educating people, but she warned that changing people's attitudes, like everything else in the field of humane work, can be slow-going. She talked candidly about her own pets who have died over the years.

"The scars are still there. I can remember every detail of their dying. With one, I knew she was dying and so I went through a process to get ready and did some homework and read some books about how to say goodbye. I went through that, did that and that was good. And the other one died in her litter box…" Sandy started to laugh and Ingrid and I joined in. "…so I didn't have to go through any of that. Nature took care of itself. I pray the rest will go like that. I have a box of ashes that I keep in my headboard and I drag them out and look at them once in a while."

Phone calls from listeners have always been an integral part of the radio show. The response to Sandy and Ingrid's comments on pet loss came quick and strong. Flashing lights on my phone indicated that people were waiting patiently to speak.

One caller, Craig, wanted to share his experience between his first and second dogs. "I had my first dog for sixteen years. That dog never left my side," Craig said. "One night he walked off. Sometimes animals know and they go off to die." Craig grieved for two years, definitely not in the mood for another dog. Then while working on a construction site one morning, Craig looked up to see a dog heading his way. "She just wandered on to the site, and of all the people working, she came up to me." Someone else took the dog for a few days, trying to place her somewhere, but had no takers. Craig decided to take the new dog home for the weekend, just to see what might happen—that was thirteen years ago. "No animal will ever replace another animal," Craig told us. "I seriously thought I'd never love another dog as much as I loved my first dog. That has proven to be false."

The most emotional call came from Monica, an older woman whose schnauzer, Charlie, died in 1993. Even now, her voice cracked as she struggled to find the words. "There's not an hour goes by that I don't mourn the little guy. Lots of people encourage me to get another pet. I'm not ready."

I asked her why not. Monica didn't mince any words. "It hurts and I don't want to go through that again. I know that I can't replace Charlie, but it hurts way too much. I don't want to go through that process of loving and losing again. I have his portrait and his ashes. Every time I go by his portrait, I say, 'Hi, Baby.' I say goodnight to him and it's just as painful five years later, incredibly painful."

Rarely had I heard so much sheer pain in a person's voice. In that one moment, my own grieving seemed miniscule compared to this woman's pain. Ingrid stepped in and encouraged Monica to consider coming to the weekly pet loss support meetings at Hospice.

Monica would not commit. "Charlie is my soul," she said. "His ashes will be buried with me. He is a moment of every part of my breath that I take, truly."

I squeezed in a last phone call from Sally, who talked about her deceased cat. Her grief at the time was so strong, Sally said she ended up having an anxiety attack and was rushed to the emergency room in an ambulance. "The doctor told me I needed to emote more," Sally explained. "I told him I had been crying all week. He said for me, that wasn't enough." Sally continued to grieve, but then realized she had learned an important lesson. "Whatever kind of craziness that happens to a person who loses a pet is OK, it's OK for them."

By this point in the program, I felt completely drained. Yet there was also a certain degree of satisfaction in seeing how meaningful the discussion had been for me, and obviously to so many of our listeners. Ingrid looked right at me as she offered one last point. "Three weeks, four weeks, is nothing, Dave. It takes a whole year to get through most of the firsts. And that year doesn't look like one of those lines that goes from the bottom left-hand side of the page to the top right-hand side of the page. It goes with a lot of ups and downs and roller coaster kind of swings."

At that moment, I didn't appreciate just how appropriate Ingrid's closing advice was for Charlotte and me. All I knew as the closing theme music swelled up was that I already wanted off the roller coaster.

THE ELEPHANT ON THE COFFEE TABLE

San Luis Obispo County Telegram-Tribune   *December 14, 1995*

Triptych and Romeo

Romeo, Romeo, where art thou ears, Romeo? A cat by any other name would smell as sweet.

Except that this beautiful blue-eyed, white feline is not like any other cat in the local hamlet of Atascadero. Romeo has no ears—aye, there's the rub. To be, or not to be? That is the question on the minds of North County Humane Society volunteers trying to find a suitable home for what everyone agrees is a very friendly, very loving, young cat.

It has not been easy. No matter how friendly, how loving this cat might be, there's always a hesitation, a reluctance, some excuse, from people who come to look Romeo over, all leading to a larger question. Which is worse—a cat with no ears, or people with no hearts?

Little is known of Romeo's tale. He's older than two, younger than five. His owner was moving and Romeo had to be left behind at the humane society's Traffic Way facility. Cancer claimed both ears when Romeo was younger. White

cats are particularly sensitive to sunlight, more likely to develop cancer than most. Surgery was successful; the cancer has not returned. Prognosis: excellent. Hearing ability: excellent. All systems go. End of story.

Not quite. The battle against cancer was relatively easy. Now Romeo has to fight ignorance and apathy. The odds are not as good. "Unfortunately, people think twice about adopting animals who appear different in some way," explains Sandy Rakestraw, president of the North County Humane Society.

The fault, dear Sandy, lies not in our stars, but in ourselves.

* * *

Long before Romeo, there was another white cat who stayed outside more than he should have. Late one night, back in 1984, he tried to cross a stretch of country road just outside Muncie, Indiana. Some joyriding kids were out and about, zooming down the road, in a hurry, going nowhere way too fast. They saw this young, white cat on the side of the road and intentionally swerved. You don't need me to paint the picture.

Yet cats have nine lives and these cretins only took one. Fortunately, a local veterinarian happened to be driving by. She witnessed everything and stopped immediately to scoop up this poor, badly injured, white cat.

The vet rushed to her office, where she performed emergency surgery. Off came the right, front leg—there was no choice. The cat was still breathing. There was hope in Hoosierland that night.

That night became a year. The three-legged cat recovered nicely, kept by the vet at her office, hanging out with all the other cats and dogs. For months, the vet lobbied in vain to find a special home for this special cat. She had no takers. No one wanted a cat with just three legs.

Then a beautiful young woman stopped by. I'm told it was love at first sight. Her name was Charlotte. She named the cat Triptych. He hopped inside her heart, and never left.

What is past is prologue.

* * *

Sandy Rakestraw picks up Romeo. His front paws cling to her, enjoying, returning the affection. "He's definitely a hugger," she says. "Don't you just love these big, blue eyes?"

Romeo almost had a home last week. A woman stopped in and seemed very tempted, but a friend talked her out of it. "You don't want that cat," the friend argued. "It will always be sick."

The attitude is rather sad. Triptych grew up to be an interesting mix of Batman and Hulk Hogan. He flies through the house with the greatest of ease; one front paw is certainly plenty for his daily wrestling bouts with our other cat, Tripper. The only thing really missing from Triptych was love. Charlotte took care of that.

Now there's actually only one thing missing from Romeo, only one thing that really matters.

To be, or not to be? That remains the question in Atascadero, where another young Romeo, like so many before him, waits quietly for his true love to come along.

EIGHT

A Certain Twinkle That Is Missing

*M*y newspaper column resumed in the *San Luis Obispo County Telegram-Tribune* on January 13, 1998. Normally the column ran on the front page of the "B" section. This time, however, editor John Moore opted to splash it across the bottom of the newspaper's front page. In part, I wrote:

> Since the fire December 14th, my wife and I have been overwhelmed with hugs, phone calls, donations, notes, letters, cards, faxes, emails and tears from both good friends and complete strangers who share our grief.... We have read every word. You have no idea of the strength you have provided. Thank you.
>
> However, we also recognize that there are those, including members of my own family, who don't understand our profound grief and sense of loss. Snap out of it. Move on. Put it behind you. Would-be advice from people who just don't understand. I won't even try to explain.
>
> Despite what happened, Charlotte and I are the first to recognize, overall, how lucky we are. Yes, we could have

been in the house, asleep, that night. We could have lost everything; instead it appears that we will salvage about half of our possessions. It's a moot point. The fire claimed everything that we really loved. Our hearts are shattered into a million tiny pieces—life will never be the same.

There is some small comfort in knowing that both donations and adoptions are up at local animal shelters since the fire. Thank you. Please don't let what happened to us keep you from bringing a pet into your home. And if you already have pets, be sure to give them a nice long hug tonight for us.

Meanwhile, Charlotte and I struggle to create some semblance of normalcy. By the end of this week, we expect to buy a house—that's a start. More animals, definitely, in time. We've both returned to work this week. Sort of. There's a certain twinkle that's missing. Tears appear without warning. Please be gentle. Thank you.

Our strategy for the last four weeks has been simple: go minute-by-minute, hour-by-hour, day-by-day. So far, so good. During our almost nonstop hugs of support, I tell my wife this: Hang on until next Christmas. I promise it will be better than this one. I promise.

Good news came, finally, in January. State Senator Jack O'Connell announced his choice for 1998 Woman of the Year from his legislative district—Charlotte Alexander. He selected her, in part, for her extensive work in the nonprofit community and for helping Cuesta College establish a new satellite campus in neighboring Paso Robles. The official ceremony to honor Charlotte and other honored women from throughout California was scheduled for early March in Sacramento. Charlotte felt genuinely moved by the award. It could not have come at a better time.

One window opens. Another one closes. Shortly after that announcement, word came that my close friend Mike Veron had died of cancer just days before his fifty-third birthday. Those last few weeks had been painful for Mike. Yet he acted more concerned about us, even insisting on donating to our fire fund. The news of his death was another sharp blow to my psyche. At least my old friend would no longer suffer, and now he and Topper could take long walks together.

Returning to work at the newspaper was difficult. Burning embers remained from the fire—I struggled to concentrate on anything else. My second newspaper column that January focused on pet loss, my third announced our decision to move to a new part of the county, and the fourth one paid tribute to Mike Veron.

In the fifth column, I attempted to describe the impact of making daily trips to a storage unit and poking around at what was left of one's life, how difficult it was to "throw away memories." After I submitted that column, the editor, John Moore, called me at home.

"I'm tempted not to run Tuesday's column," he said.

I was surprised. "Why not?"

"You need to move on, David," John replied. "Enough is enough. Time for fresh topics."

"I thought I was supposed to share my personal feelings."

Short pause on the other end. "We'll run this one, but no more," John responded. "Move on, OK?"

Landlord Bill wanted us back on Pacific Street. Things had gone smoothly with the insurance company and renovation began quickly.

In a matter of weeks, the house would be ready to occupy, good as new. Bill made it known that it was ours for the asking.

Pacific Street had been our dream situation. A unique little house bordering the edge of downtown, putting us close to movies, to restaurants and to work. We had been so happy there. Yet our decision took about ten seconds. That's how quickly the four-legged ghosts started materializing in our minds. My voice started cracking as I tried to explain things in a phone call.

"We can't, Bill. There's just no way."

He understood, of course. I heard a few tears on his end. We quickly shifted to other topics. A promise of lunch on the horizon. Yes, of course, we'd stay in touch—definitely. In the back of my mind, I began to wonder about where Charlotte and I would go next.

San Luis Obispo County, roughly the size of Delaware, has a great cultural and physical divide. Just north of San Luis Obispo, Highway 101 snakes up along the ever-winding Cuesta grade, eventually dumping drivers out into the flatlands of Atascadero, a city whose name supposedly translates into "mud hole." A distinct Midwestern flavor hangs in the air, hovering over the endless stretch of fast food joints, strip mini-malls, and churches. It's only about a fifteen-minute drive from San Luis Obispo, but all that seems light years away. Atascadero is not the California one sees on postcards. Palm trees give way to scrubby oaks and urban activity fades away. The environment is more rural, more quiet. No partying college students in Atascadero. August heat often tops out at a sizzling 110—in the shade.

In this quiet mud hole, we decided to begin anew and buy a house, hoping somehow that this would get our lives back on track. Our new home, graced with a contemporary design, was nestled in a small residential tract where all the houses seemed constructed from the same mold. Yet there were distinct advantages to the new house. Much larger in size. All new appliances and utilities. No prior occupant. Nice backyard, fenced in. Stucco on the inside. Stucco on the outside. Wall-to-wall carpeting. Plenty of skylights. A nice sterile atmosphere. This was as far away from the little house on Pacific Street as we could get in many ways.

Moving to Atascadero became a turning point for us, because now our daily routines would be completely different. New streets to drive on. New stores. A complete change of scenery. No painful memories of Pacific Street to face every morning. We initially adjusted to an environment without loved ones by opting to create a new environment.

The process of replacement continued inside the house as well. We bought new furniture and personal belongings, as needed. I continued focusing on the clean-up process, going through whatever we had salvaged from the fire. Almost every day I sorted through the boxes at the storage unit, each one a difficult memory. We had to decide what stayed to be cleaned and what had to be thrown out. When in doubt, I tossed it.

There quickly came the point where I had to wonder which scenario was worse: Coming home to find the house completely burned to the ground and losing everything; or coming home to a damaged house and then having to sift through everything, each damaged item bringing a new heartache.

Initially, we displayed very little in the new house. Nothing hung on the walls and no photos could be found. The sole exception was Jeff Blue's photo of Topper and me that Charlotte allowed me to hang in the foyer. I wanted that gentle reminder every time I left the house. Only after several weeks did I finally clear off a single bookshelf in our rear office to display photos of Topper, Triptych, Tripper, Trio, and Tess. It was time to honor them again.

At the same time, all the new clothes and new furniture and new appliances do not a home make. That certain twinkle was still missing. There were no pets in our lives. We were still very much alone.

The absence of animal companions was killing us daily—a long, steady, painful drip-drip-drip of emptiness. Our pain was so great that we had to be especially careful to avoid the pet supply aisle when we did the grocery shopping. One night, we accidentally stepped into the aisle and instantly backed away when we saw all the cat and dog food. That's how fragile we had become.

Immediately after the fire, offers of new pets flooded our way. Everyone wanted to give us one of their dogs or cats. "Not now, thank you," we pleaded. We will know when it's time, we agreed. Only then would the search begin.

Things came to a head on a Monday night in late January. On the surface, there appeared to be many positive signs for us. The new house was available and we could begin moving. Both of us had returned to work. Thanks to a large community fund, we had kept our heads above water. Still, none of the good news could keep us from our zombie-like existence. As Ingrid Pires predicted, Charlotte and I were on a speeding roller coaster and the ride was definitely taking its toll.

Laying in bed together in the upstairs loft of the temporary house, Charlotte began crying. It could just as easily have been me—hell, the night before it probably had been. I pulled her towards me, but there was no need to ask what was wrong. Through her muffled tears, Charlotte started talking about Triptych and Tripper and Trio and how much she missed them. This conversation had taken place so many times, in so many different forms, during the last five weeks, but this time, I silently snapped, unable to bear hearing my wife in such pain.

I made a silent vow. *Enough. No more.* No, I couldn't bring back the five that we had lost, but neither one of us could go a single day longer without some kind of animal companion in our lives. The fire claimed many things, but not our commitment and love for animals that was so realized when we rescued Tess in November. Other animals were waiting. Other animals needed to be loved.

And, I realized, holding Charlotte as tightly as I could, we needed to be loved, in return.

San Luis Obispo County Telegram-Tribune   December 24, 1992

Ho Ho: The Dog Who Saved Christmas

'Twas well after midnight. Half-asleep in my warm bed, quietly drifting towards dreamland, I heard something stir in the dark.

On came the light and I shot up with concern, only to discover my dog Topper sitting quietly at the foot of the bed. He was staring at me, silently waiting. The dog seemed frozen in place, a canine statue deserving to be in some museum, not waiting here in our bedroom.

I knew immediately what he wanted. "Forget it, Topper," I growled. "No way. I'm trying to sleep." But Topper would not budge. He remained at the foot of the bed, staring at me as if I was a thick slab of juicy prime rib.

I continued to resist. "Go to bed, Topper. Not tonight."

Charlotte began stirring next to me. The dog ignored her, keeping his focus directly on me. "What's wrong with Topper?" Charlotte muttered, still half-asleep. "Does he need to go out?"

"He's fine. I know what he wants. And the answer is still n-o, no."

Then Topper flashed that look of complete innocence as he played his trump card. Up came his left paw on the bed. When it comes to begging, this dog has no shame. It was useless to resist.

Mumbling, grumbling, stumbling, I slipped on my bathrobe and followed Topper down the hallway, through the kitchen and into the family room. The lights were already on—somebody knew to expect me.

Actually there were six in all, gathered quietly around Topper, in front of the Christmas tree, just as I had expected. I recognized most of them from the neighborhood.

Baron, the fierce-looking German shepherd, had been here before. There was no mistaking Cody, the giant sheepdog. Lucky, the brown cocker spaniel, came from next door. Max was a breed of dubious mix and equally dubious home. Daisy, the beautiful golden retriever, belonged up the street. Topper hovered over the young beagle, whom I believe was named Bonnie.

There I stood in the family room with seven dogs and fourteen eager eyes staring up at me, bursting with excitement and anticipation.

"Let me guess," I said to the dogs. "You came to hear the story, didn't you?"

Immediately, seven tails began pounding on the carpet in a canine chorus of approval. There was no turning back. Breathing a heavy sigh, I shrugged my surrender. "Gather 'round," I told my visitors as I wearily plopped down on the couch. "And remember—no barking. No drooling. No begging."

Lucky leaped up on my lap. The other dogs dropped quietly near my feet as I began to share the story that Topper has made me tell so many other dogs over so many years.

The story of Ho Ho, the dog who saved Christmas.

* * *

Christmas Eve at the North Pole. Everything was falling into place on that crisp midnight clear. The elves had been working hard all year in Santa's workshop, and finally, all the wonderful new toys were ready to go. Into the sleigh went the brightly wrapped presents, jammed together so tightly that the poor sleigh threatened to burst.

A proud and confident Santa Claus stood in the doorway, looking over his list one last time. Oh, he knew who had been naughty, and who had been nice. It was time again to visit with all the good little girls and good little boys around the world. He sniffed with pleasure at the Christmas cookies Mrs. Claus had baked especially for the trip—what a glorious night this would be, Santa thought.

The mighty reindeer were ready, as well. Prancer, Blitzen and Rudolph, too. They had been exercising for weeks, getting in shape for this oh-so-special trip. One last meal, and they would be ready to go.

All at the North Pole seemed to be as it had for years. Soon all the children around the world would be happy; Santa was on his way.

But it was not to be. The barn door suddenly flew open and out rushed a clearly upset Mrs. Claus, trying her best not to slip on the ice. "Santa! Santa! Come quickly! Hurry, Santa!" she cried.

Santa dropped his Christmas list and cookies, hurrying towards the barn to join his dear wife. "What is it? What's wrong?" he demanded to know.

Mrs. Claus was too upset, too shocked to speak. She could only point in horror at the open barn door. Santa, now joined by his curious elves, peeked inside.

They froze in their tracks at what they found.

There were all of Santa's reindeer—Prancer and Comet and Dasher, too. All lying on the ground, holding their stomachs in pain. Aghast, Santa went to his fallen reindeer. "Rudolph? Blitzen? Can this be? What has happened to my faithful reindeer?"

The reindeer, however, were in too much agony to speak. Only Dasher could make any sense as he feebly lifted his head. "Our dinner, Santa. The food was so bad," the weakened reindeer explained. "We're all so very sick, too sick to move."

The reindeer too sick to move? On Christmas Eve?

Poor Santa couldn't believe what he was hearing. And then he saw all the empty Polar Bear pizza boxes scattered among the straw. How many times had he warned the reindeer about pizza on Christmas Eve? Santa knew instantly that all was lost. Distraught and confused, he pushed the elves aside and ran out of the barn, dashing alone into the starry, cold North Pole night.

He wandered in the snow, unable to accept what had happened. What about all the toys that had to be delivered? What about all the children who were waiting for Santa Claus?

Santa stared up at the stars and shook his fist in anger, trying to hold back his tears. "What am I to do?" he bellowed at the sky. "Someone tell me what I'm supposed to do! There must be a Christmas!"

The stars fell silent. Santa dropped to his knees in the snow. It was useless. There would be no Christmas this year.

Then the silence of the night was broken by the ever-so-soft jingling of bells in the distance. Santa jumped to his feet—the reindeer must be healthy again, he thought. All is well!

But his excitement quickly turned to disappointment as the bells came closer.

They didn't belong to any of the reindeer. It was only Ho Ho, Santa's brown-and-white dog, who had come out in search of his master.

Santa had found Ho Ho a few years before, in the middle of a fierce winter storm that roared across Montana. Near death, poor Ho Ho had been harshly abandoned in the cold by an uncaring family. Santa brought the young dog home to the North Pole where Mrs. Claus gently nursed him back to health. She insisted that the dog remain with the family.

Now Santa had never owned a dog before. As a result, no one was quite sure what to do with Ho Ho. The protective and jealous elves kept him away from the toy shop. Santa was usually too busy working on his Christmas list and letters to spend much time with his new dog.

And the reindeer? Well, they wanted nothing to do with a dog. They laughed and laughed about Ho Ho, always teasing him, never, ever letting the dog join in any of their silly reindeer games.

So Ho Ho spent most of his time curled up quietly on the floor near Mrs. Claus, hoping for the year that he, too, could help bring Christmas. On this night, however, all Ho Ho could do was leap up on his hind legs and begin licking his master's face. Santa tearfully hugged his loyal companion.

"All is lost, dear, sweet Ho Ho," Santa whispered softly. "If only you were a reindeer, my four-legged friend."

Ho Ho cocked his head one way, then the other. He grabbed Santa's red coat in his teeth, and started pulling, forcing a bewildered Santa to follow. Ho Ho barked twice, his voice echoing off the surrounding snow banks.

Santa couldn't understand his excited dog. "What is it, Ho Ho? What are you trying to tell me?"

Another loud bark was the answer. Ho Ho turned and raced eagerly back towards Santa's sleigh. Santa hesitated, then followed, curious about what his dog was doing.

Back at the sleigh, the worried elves and the sick reindeer gathered around, drawn by Ho Ho's loud barking. Mrs. Claus clutched her concerned husband's arm. They all watched in disbelief as Ho Ho picked up the sleigh's leather harness in his teeth and tried to pull with every ounce of strength he could manage.

Nothing happened. Still determined, Ho Ho tried again. This time, he lost his balance and plopped face-first in the snow. The elves laughed. The reindeer laughed. Even Mrs. Claus was forced to smile through her tears. Santa shook his head as he walked over to his dog.

"There, there, poor Ho Ho," Santa said, in the kindest voice he could muster. "You mean well, but I'm afraid nothing can help us now."

Ho Ho ignored the laughter. He sprang to his feet—into the air his nose did go. And what a sound emerged—a shrill howl that filled the December night.

Silence. Ho Ho tried again. More silence, except for the continued boisterous laughter from the elves and reindeer.

One last time, Ho Ho tried. He took a deep breath and let loose with all the energy he could summon.

Nothing. Poor, poor Ho Ho. What was this silly dog trying to prove?

And then, off in the distance, another howl was suddenly heard. All eyes turned south, towards the rumbling swirl of snow quickly heading their way.

One by one, the dogs arrived at the North Pole. There was a sheepdog, a cocker spaniel, and a German shepherd, too. The beagle came next, the golden retriever nipped closely at her heels. Eight in all, the dogs pulled up in front of Santa. They were panting in excitement, their tails wagging in delight.

"We are here to bring Christmas, Santa," they shouted in unison.

"But you are just dogs," an astonished Santa replied. "What can you possibly do?"

The dogs responded by lining up in strict formation in front of the sleigh. Ho Ho assumed the lead position. His eyes locked lovingly on Santa.

"You once saved me, Santa, now let me save you."

Clearly flabbergasted, Santa hesitated for but a second. He saw the look of shock registered on his wife. The elves were equally speechless. They looked at Ho Ho and then at Santa. And then back at Ho Ho. They all knew the answer.

So the elves quickly scrambled around the sleigh, securing the harness on this new team of four-legged helpers. Mrs. Claus gave her husband a warm embrace for luck. Looking rather indignant, the stunned reindeer began shaking their heads furiously and pounding their hoofs to protest, but Santa paid them no heed.

He climbed into his sleigh and a very excited Santa Claus thundered with joy. "On sheepdog! On German shepherd! On beagle and golden retriever! And Ho Ho, my dear and beloved dog, won't you guide my sleigh tonight?"

A chorus of enthusiastic barking answered Santa. Up, up, and away went the sleigh, as the dogs continued barking, as their tails continued wagging.

And just as Santa disappeared into the clouds that special Christmas Eve, he was heard to proclaim. "Thanks to the dogs, there will be a Christmas this year, after all! Ho ho ho!"

* * *

There was no barking in the family room. No panting. No drooling. Not tonight. All seven dogs remained perfectly still, hanging on my every word.

"So you see," I said softly. "Dogs are a very important part of Christmas. You're very, very, very special. All of you. Don't let anyone ever tell you differently."

Topper flashed his famous see-I-told-you-so look to the other dogs. They didn't need convincing.

Now it was really time for bed; time for these dogs to be on their way. I slipped each one a biscuit as they floated out our front door, excitedly scampering off into the night, no doubt in search of other dogs they could share this story with. Finally, I could get some sleep.

I fell back into bed and hugged my pillow, determined to dream about anything other than howling dogs and pizza-eating reindeer.

Then I heard more movement in the dark. Now what? I switched on the light and glared down at the foot of the bed.

There was Triptych, our white three-legged cat, staring at me. His left paw perched up on the bed.

"Forget it," I barked. "Don't even think about it."

NINE

Starting Over

When I first went for Topper in January 1984, I was guided strictly by my heart. There was no rhyme nor reason to my choice. He was The One—I just knew it. I never dreamed that there would eventually be five animals in my life, but in each of those cases, my heart did the talking. In each case, there emerged an indelibly strong connection.

Topper, Triptych, Tripper, Trio, and Tess were unique. Charlotte and I knew from the outset that they never could be replaced. However, it didn't take long for us to realize that we needed to have new animals in our lives.

Charlotte claims that I have a special gift. She has always been amazed by my ability to walk through an animal shelter and connect with a great dog or a cat. There's no magic formula. I never visit a shelter with any particular wish list. Besides, I don't believe that we choose animals. They choose us. All we had to do was to be alert and look for a sign.

TRISTAN – After that anguished, lonely Monday night, I drove out the next afternoon to Woods Humane Society, a shelter just on the outskirts of San Luis Obispo. Our friend Aleida Lund, the executive director at the time, cleared her jammed schedule to personally guide me through the always-crowded cat room.

"What do you have in mind, David?' Aleida asked.

I shrugged. "Beats me. All I know is that I'm not going home tonight without a cat. For Charlotte."

For Charlotte? Yeah, right, Dave. It's for Charlotte.

Aleida played along, obviously knowing better. The available cats weren't as cooperative, making absolutely no effort to help their cause. Dozens of pairs of eyes stared blankly at me through the wire cages. Who are you? What do you want? But there was no sign. Cat after cat was brought out of the cage. Cat after cat went back inside the cage. I began to wonder if I should have even come to the shelter.

Then the outside door blew open and a staff member whisked inside with a beautiful orange-and-white marmalade cradled in her arms. The cat was about a year old and seemingly healthy. He had just been dropped off by a woman from San Luis Obispo. She had found him right before Christmas and kept him for awhile, but the woman simply had too many cats. I watched as Aleida gently slid him into an empty steel cage.

"He needs a name," said Aleida. She looked at the cat. Then she looked at me. "Hey, let's call him Dave." Aleida was serious.

I didn't know anything about marmalade cats, but a cosmic connection was beginning to develop. This cat and I both show up at the shelter at the same time? I'm looking for a cat. He's looking for a home. To me, this was a sign.

"How 'bout this guy?" I casually asked. "He looks like a great cat."

"Sure, sure," replied Aleida. "This is a great cat."

There's a good chance that this marmalade named Dave set a record for adoption, having spent less than fifteen minutes in the shelter. After the quick paperwork, I drove directly out to Cuesta College, trying to prep a cat I hardly knew for the role of a lifetime.

"I don't want to put any pressure on you, Mr. Cat, but you

certainly have your work cut out for you," I warned as I worried about whether or not I was doing the right thing.

Any doubt vanished when I saw Charlotte's reaction. The cat wandered into her office (with a little coaxing from me in the hallway). She stopped working and began chatting up the cat. When Charlotte scooped him up and held him in her arms, I wasn't sure she would ever let go. Two days later, we agreed on the name Tristan. His impact on us was immediate. Having a pet in the house again quickly stabilized us. The eerie solitude vanished and there was no more being home alone.

Count: One cat. Zero dogs.

CHARLES FOSTER KANINE – Originally his name was Harley and despite being a purebred basset hound, this dog has led anything but a royal life. He had four different families in slightly more than three years, moving from Los Angeles to the Central Coast. The last family had kept him barely a week and he lost a chunk off the bridge of his nose to a jealous rottweiler already in the house. And then Harley committed the Big No-No—trying to steal food off the table. He was exiled back to the Woods Humane Society Shelter, banned for bad behavior. Poor guy—born a prince, sentenced to live as a pauper.

The basset was strictly Charlotte's idea. I knew nothing about the breed. The fact that he was purebred impressed me even less. But hard-luck Harley obviously needed a good home. Charlotte promised—she promised—to take care of him. And he appeared so unlike Topper on every level. I saw that as a big plus. Besides, have you ever tried to say no to your spouse at an animal shelter? Still, I insisted on one condition: No dogs named Harley.

The drooling, overly energetic basset hound came to Atascadero as Charles Foster Kanine, a.k.a. Charlie. A local veterinarian later wrote to us, recalling that she had never treated a basset that didn't have a human name.

Count: One cat. One dog.

EMMA – Emma is a "tortie." Maybe three years old, maybe older. She was hit by a car and left for dead by the side of the road. A guardian angel found her and rushed her to the veterinarian. The doctor did what he could, but this cat had suffered some degree of permanent brain damage. Things would always be a little "off" for her. The cat would be distant and aloof, certainly not likely to respond to much.

After recovering, the cat was taken in by the North County Humane Society and named Jo Anne. She quickly discovered a favorite perch on top of the shelter's washing machine. Jo Anne would sit there all day, we theorize, enjoying the sensation of the vibrating washer. She sat there week after week, staring off into space, apparently shell-shocked from the accident. People ignored her, wanting more in a cat. Then in walked Charlotte. The rest is history.

Count: Two cats. One dog.

EARL GREY – In every batch of household pets, there's always one with an attitude. It used to be Tripper. Now it would be this new guy, the gray tabby named Turtle.

He belonged indirectly to Leah Bauer, an assistant to Dr. Knighton. She had raised Turtle from birth, eventually placing him with a friend. Leah is a stickler on adoptions. If things don't work out, for whatever reason, the person has to sign a piece of paper promising to return the animal to Leah.

For some mysterious reason, the man who had Turtle decided after about a year that he didn't want the cat anymore. So he stashed the cat in a cage and dumped it on Leah's front porch without warning. Leah wasn't around, so poor Turtle remained trapped in the cage for more than twelve hours, much of that in a constant cold downpour.

Leah needed a new home for Turtle and she immediately thought of us. We didn't commit right away. Charlotte and I hadn't really talked about how many new pets we wanted. Admittedly, there was some concern about getting so many pets, so quickly. After all, the fire had only been six weeks ago. A persistent Leah kept dropping hints and leaving messages, working us like an Amway salesperson. Charlotte finally swung by her house one night after work.

Turtle came home to Atascadero that same night, announcing his arrival with hiss after hiss directed at Tristan and Emma.

"Can we keep him?" Charlotte asked, pretending that the decision had not already been made.

"Of course, we can," I replied, pretending that I had any say in this. "If we can change the name." There I went again, ranting about names. "I really don't want a cat named Turtle."

Turtle became Earl Grey.

Count: Three cats. One dog.

TANNER – Every Friday morning on my radio show, there's a brief pet segment featuring a dog or cat up for adoption. The success rate is fairly high, but it's risky hosting a show with all these sweet, lovable, available, needy animals dropping by. It tears my heart out to see what some people have done to some animals. I want to help them all and take every one home, but that's not realistic. The best I can do is to publicize their plight and hope some caring family or individual is listening.

Tanner's heritage was a mystery. Collie? Whippet? Borzoi? Curly-haired retriever? He was the ultimate Heinz 57 dog, another county pound dog short on time. The comparison was unavoidable. Here was a brown-and-white dog named Tanner. I had just lost a brown-and-white dog named Topper. For me, this was a sign—Tanner was a Las Vegas casino marquee at midnight, flashing brightly in my eyes.

Charlotte and I had talked about getting a second dog. A regret I always had with Topper was that I never got him a companion dog. I didn't want to repeat that mistake. Charles Foster Kanine suddenly had a new playmate named Tanner.

Count: Three cats. Two dogs.

ALEXANDER, REUBEN, AND ROMEO – Three cats. Two dogs. Almost overnight, Charlotte and I were back where we started before Christmas. Of course, this was a completely different menagerie of pets. Tanner and Charlie fought constantly in those early weeks together, trying to establish territory. Earl Grey kept hissing. I kept hissing, wondering if this had been right, dashing out in the rain like Noah and rounding up animals just because we didn't want to face the loneliness of the morning.

But what was done, was done. We had stepped forward. We will take these five, we pledged. This would all work out eventually. However, one thing rapidly became clear. Five was enough. No more.

Then Larry Kahn appeared on my radio show in early March, a Wednesday as I recall. Larry runs the small volunteer group that works with the county animal facility. Given the high annual kill rate, it's difficult to call it a shelter. Our discussion was only meant to be about Larry and the volunteers, but he just couldn't resist a possible opportunity to help an animal. He arrived at the radio station with an absolutely gorgeous calico and an eleventh-hour appeal. Her time was running out. Someone please help.

Our interview that morning ran for fifty-five minutes. I kept glancing at the cat, totally enthralled by her charm and beauty. She spent most of the time near Larry, purring softly, letting him stroke her long hair. What a beautiful cat, I thought. Good choice, Larry. Somebody will come for her.

I called the office later that afternoon, just to be sure. To both my surprise and alarm, no one had come for the calico. Not even one single phone call. I immediately called Charlotte and asked her to check things out on her way home.

"Just take a look at her," I urged. "See what you think."

Sending Charlotte to any animal facility is like sending a child to the candy store. Neither one is likely to return empty handed.

Charlotte signed the papers that night. No, this wasn't a commitment to keep her. We just wanted to keep the cat alive until we could figure something out. The cat was transported to Los Osos for spaying by Dr. Knighton, which gave us a few days to devise a plan. That was until a bemused Dr. Knighton called the next morning. First, he announced, the cat had a respiratory infection, ruling out any surgery. More importantly, he added, there was another complication. The calico was pregnant, as in due-any-day pregnant.

The cat would have to come home to Atascadero and recuperate. We set her up in the middle bedroom, away from the other animals, but she wasn't alone for long. Three days later, Charlotte and I walked in to discover that our new calico had company. One-two-three-four finger-sized kittens were nursing on Mom. We were no longer living in a house. Our home had become a no-kill shelter.

My friends at the county pound later told me that if the kittens had been born a few days earlier, they would have been euthanized along with the mother. I shuddered at the news. We had lost five animal companions in December. Now here we were, saving five in March.

Charlotte named the mother Desiree, but steadfastly refused to name the kittens. "If you name the kittens, you have to keep them," my wife, the cat expert, declared. They stayed with us for the next three months: a marmalade, a calico, and two smoke-gray kittens. Everyone asked if they could adopt one so we created a waiting list. No need to worry, or so we thought.

Desiree would eventually go to live with Charlotte's mother in Indianapolis. We also found a wonderful home for the calico kitten. Two taken care of. Then our luck ran out—or, depending on your viewpoint, our luck began. All the people who once wanted one of our kittens suddenly developed excuses for not taking one. Interested strangers who called did not sound like good candidates for adopting a kitten.

Meanwhile, Tristan had started playing the role of cat uncle to the three remaining kittens, bonding with them, and spending a great deal of time together. The longer they stayed, the harder it was to say goodbye.

Somewhere along the way, another epiphany enlightened our lives. This is what mattered to us—these cats and dogs and kittens who had wandered into our lives. This is what we really cared about—not our jobs or meaningless material goods. These kittens were another important sign.

The marmalade kitten became Reuben. We named the smoky twins Alexander and Romeo.

Count: Three cats. Three kittens. Two dogs.

HANNAH – We certainly had our hands full with all these new animals invading our house. They clearly weren't enough to stop the grief we continued to feel for Topper, Triptych, Tripper, Trio, and Tess. However, I can't imagine what it would have been like without the new group around. They were making it easier to inch forward.

Charlotte flew back to Indianapolis in June to visit her mother and to take Desiree to her new home. That week was the longest we had been apart since the fire. It felt strange not having her around. Charlotte's birthday was coming up towards the end of June and I wanted to get her something special.

Maybe that's why I drove out to the North County Humane Society shelter one afternoon that week. Here we were with a house full of pets and I thought of getting still another one. Perhaps my mind was on poor Trio who had been such a great Christmas gift for Charlotte. No rational explanation can be offered.

The Atascadero shelter is located in an old geodesic dome-shaped house. That day, cage after cage was jammed with the latest ravages of the kitten season. I found one young male in the kitten room that I quickly became quite fond of. He leaped right over to me and started playing with my index finger. I could already picture him with Romeo or Tristan. *This guy would fit right in*, I told myself. He's healthy and a perfect match. He had Happy Birthday written all over him.

I kept looking around, in no particular hurry. My prime candidate was stashed in the back of my mind. Then I stepped into the tiny isolation ward—just curious, I guess. There they were in the upper cage on the left-hand side. Three kittens who had been brought in that very morning, abandoned in a cardboard box along a busy highway. A fourth kitten had been killed by a car; a fifth had run away.

The tiny black kitten with the white specks, barely a month old, caught my attention. There was nothing left of her right eye, the result of a severe infection. She would require surgery. The shelter manager warned me that it could be expensive. Then I thought about the playful, healthy kitten in the other room—but only for a second. He would find a home. This one-eyed kitten would have a tougher time.

So I drove home and called Charlotte in Indianapolis and told her about the one-eyed ray of hope. I didn't even have to ask. Hannah would be waiting when Charlotte came home.

Count: Three cats. Four kittens. Two dogs.

San Luis Obispo County Telegram-Tribune   March 30, 1995

Raindrops Keep Falling On My Tail

I hope you're able to read this in warm, bright sunshine, because that will mean the recent torrential rains have finally stopped.

It's raining—again—as I write this. Rain and more rain. I'm beginning to wonder if the sun just gave up and joined everyone else currently fleeing California. Looking out my window, I half-expect the ark to float by any minute now. Charlotte and I can tough it out. But I worry about Topper.

Triptych, ever the indoor cat, can fend for himself. After all, he really doesn't feel the need to venture outside. Rain or shine, he's quite content.

Topper is a different story. He just stares. And stares. And stares. At the front door. Outside the living room window. Staring, and sighing, listening to the constant, thundering rain, no doubt wondering how long this will continue. Sensing somehow that, once again, there will be no trip to the beach today. Silently accepting his fate to be stuck once again inside a cold house with a sleeping cat for another day.

Leaving me to pose the question that has forever plagued concerned dog owners: What do you do with your dog when it rains?

* * *

We're sitting in my truck, parked next to the empty field in Los Osos. At least, I think that's where we are. I can hardly see anything through the downpour. The rain pounds on my windows.

Topper sits next to me, with no trace of his normal enthusiasm. I must have a hundred layers of warm clothing on me, but that doesn't matter. I'm not the one planning on stepping outside. Leaning in front of Topper, I push his door open. The rain quickly sprays inside.

"Outside, Topper," I command. "Go do your thing."

The dog hesitates. I add more authority to my voice the second time. "C'mon, Topper. Go." Topper reluctantly jumps outside, moving with all the energy of a death row prisoner. But he stays close to the truck, eyes fixed back on me.

"Go-Go-Go," I yell in my best Bobby Knight.

Instead, Topper stays-stays-stays, waiting patiently in the rain, water splattering all around. Waiting for me. Staring at me.

I command. I threaten. I cajole. I beg. I curse. No good. The dog won't budge.

So I zip up my yellow hood and step out of the truck. Right into a puddle.

"Make it quick," I mutter.

* * *

I call Topper down to the garage. Charlotte tags along, concerned that I'm even thinking of going outside in the storm.

My wife is surprised to find our garage empty. I've moved both my truck and her Tracer out on the street.

"What's going on?" she asks.

The answer is the tennis ball clutched in my right hand. "Exercise," I explain.

And with the first bounce of the ball off the far wall, our garage is magically transformed into the new training center for the canine Olympics.

"Get it, Topper," I urge. "Get the ball."

Topper responds, not with a bang, but a waddle, leisurely walking over in the semi-direction of the ball. He watches with a half-curiosity as the ball rolls to a stop in front of the washing machine. The dog sniffs at the ball and glances back over towards Charlotte and me with one of those Hey-What-Now-Dave? expressions.

"Maybe you should come inside, now," my wife suggests.

* * *

It's time to leave for work. The rain seems unending as I reach inside the hall closet for my warmest jacket. Topper strategically places himself directly between myself and the stairway leading down to the garage. Message understood.

"No way," I say in my firmest voice. "You can't come with me. It's still raining outside."

Topper responds by placing his head down between his front paws, feigning shame for even bringing up the issue. Suddenly, I'm an attorney arguing before the Canine Supreme Court, trying in vain to mix common sense with dog logic.

"You'll just have to sit in the truck. Alone. For hours. Believe me, you're better off staying here with Triptych. I'll even leave the TV on."

Topper reluctantly lets me pass, but there is no mistaking that hurt look in his eyes, feeling like he had just learned that Lassie was seeing another dog. He delights in trying to make me feel guilty for leaving him behind. It follows me like the rain, all the way into work.

* * *

Topper stretches out on the tattered living room couch, now in danger of becoming a certifiable couch biscuit. He sighs once, then again for emphasis, loud enough to be heard in Bakersfield as the latest storm angrily bounces over the picture window above him.

Another day not spent at the beach. Another day not chasing other sniffing, tail-wagging dogs. Another day not meeting people who'll smother him with attention and affection.

The forecast calls for sunny skies tomorrow. Perhaps. All we can do is wait, and see. For there's really very little else to do with a dog in the rain except to quietly but forcefully pray to the Rain Gods.

Rain, rain, go away.
Come back again some
other day.
Please give my dog a
chance to play.
For he has miles to go
before he sleeps.
Miles, with me, before
he sleeps.

TEN

Learning To Heal

Laguna Lake Park, just minutes from downtown San Luis Obispo, is acre upon acre of open space, an inviting mix of eucalyptus trees, water, and lush green pastures that wrap around the foothills of nearby San Luis Mountain. Paragliders and hikers share the well-worn trails. And there are dogs everywhere.

This park was Topper's second home for years. Two, three, four times a day, rain or shine, we would be at the park. There wasn't a blade of grass left unsniffed, or a spot he failed to mark. Tess enjoyed a slice of canine heaven for about three weeks, bouncing along the trails at high energy, trying to encourage Topper to keep up. What a time they had together at Laguna Lake.

Those days are gone. Now I was in a new house, in a new town, with two new dogs, and one old question—where do I walk my dogs? Charlie and Tanner always seemed anxious to play. Our backyard would not be enough to contain them. They needed to run. But where?

One Sunday morning, I loaded them into my truck and made the twenty-minute drive to Laguna Lake. They needed to go somewhere, I decided, but what was I thinking?

Images of Topper and Tess greeted us the moment I swung through the main entrance to the park. I pressed ahead, thinking everything would be OK. After parking, I leashed the dogs and we marched along an all-too-familiar grove of eucalyptus trees, towards the beginning of a major trail. Out of habit, I let an equally excited Charlie and Tanner off their leashes. And away they went, Peter Fonda and Dennis Hopper in search of America, born to be wild.

We wandered the first few hundred yards without incident, sticking to higher ground, trying to avoid other dogs. Charlie and Tanner, pleased with this new freedom, tried to stay on good behavior. I stopped to sit on a small rock formation and take in the majestic view, just like on so many previous walks. All I could see were Topper and Tess.

What the hell am I doing here? I sighed.

There wasn't much chance to ponder. A pair of overly eager German shepherds magically appeared on the scene, way ahead of their owner, heading directly for Tanner and Charlie. My dogs decided to meet them halfway.

"Charlie! Tanner!" I yelled, scrambling down the trail, trying to catch up. It was pointless. Charlie paused long enough to exchange greetings with the shepherds before picking up a different scent. My basset hound galloped off, charging straight back towards the parking lot.

"Charlie!!!"

Tanner was easy to catch within minutes. While I clipped on his leash, I tried to keep Charlie in sight. He seemed halfway to Mexico by now. The more I called, the farther he ran. We followed that determined dog for the next ten minutes. Through the eucalyptus grove, past the rotary barbecue pit, and on to the parking lot. Then Charlie ran back through the barbecue pit.

My right boot came untied. I kept running, praying that no cars would speed by. More shouting. More running. Finally, the chase ended only when Charlie mistakenly ran out on to the small metal pier jutting directly into Laguna Lake. Trapped. Drooling. Excited. He was very pleased with himself as he flashed that gee-that-was-fun look.

Huffing and puffing, woefully out of shape, I clipped on Charlie's leash, feeling like a sheriff finally catching his long-sought fugitive.

I felt so helpless, so frustrated. *Topper and Tess never would have done this. They always listened to me.* That's all I could think about as I gasped for breath, stupidly blaming my new dogs for just being dogs. As I stood on that metal dock, with the two leashes tangled together, Tanner and Charlie pulled me in separate directions. For a fleeting moment, I felt tempted to just jump.

What a big mistake to come here. What was I thinking, expecting the experience to be the same? With an air of surrender, I hurriedly hustled Charlie and Tanner into the truck and raced home to Atascadero. Laguna Lake belonged to Topper and Tess. Charlie, Tanner and I would have to find somewhere else to take our walks.

This incident made me reconsider Heilmann Park. I had never been there prior to moving to Atascadero, but after the debacle at Laguna Lake, it was definitely time for a visit. The next afternoon, I loaded Charlie and Tanner back in the truck, not knowing what to expect from this new park.

Though certainly not as big as Laguna Lake, Heilmann Park unfolded into an inviting mix of oak trees, tennis courts, ravines, and a multitude of hiking paths that snaked all the way back to the border of the public golf course. All of this was less than one block off the main street in town.

Initially, I was struck by how quiet the park was. Friends had told me the place is usually empty. They were right, this was a ghost park. Most locals tended to favor Atascadero Lake, complete with a zoo and picnic area, on the other side of town.

Pulling into the parking space, I saw how eager Charlie and Tanner looked as they stuck their heads out the open window. I became a little excited myself. *How did I miss this place? Boy, Topper would love this. I can't believe I never brought him here.* Once again, I caught myself in that Topper mindset.

Heilmann Park would work just fine—virgin territory waiting to be discovered, new memories waiting to be created. This time, Charlie would stay safely secured on the leash. From this point on, I treated my basset like a death row convict, ready to bolt at any moment with nothing to lose. These were new beginnings.

Those early weeks with the new dogs were almost enough to send me back into regular therapy sessions. Several local therapists did contact us after the fire, each offering a supportive ear if Charlotte or I needed to talk. I'm no stranger to the process, having long sought professional help for my on-going battle against depression. As things began to settle in Atascadero, I called up Mary Speidell and asked for an appointment. If anyone understood what I was going through, she would.

Mary had lost her dog, the love of her life, a few years back. At the time, she and her husband were living on a busy residential street in San Luis Obispo. Their dog suddenly bolted out into the street and was killed by an on-coming car as Mary watched in horror. Today, the couple live in the country, as far away from traffic as possible, as far away from that other house on the busy street. Years later, Mary still grieves for her dog.

So I returned to the familiar blue couch in the familiar upstairs office and listened as Mary advised me that the healing process would be long and emotionally draining. There was no magic wand. Would I consider medication? No, no, thank you—I'll stick to the St. John's Wort.

"I'm living in a stucco tract house," I complained at one point. "We don't have anything hanging on the walls. It's so sterile."

"That's because you see it as a hospital, not a home," Mary replied. "You're still recovering. You'll know when it's time to hang things on the walls again. It all takes time. Give it time."

Then she smiled. "I'm looking forward to reading your book about all this, David."

The statement caught me by surprise. "Book? What book?" I asked.

"Oh, the book I think you're getting ready to write."

Mary and I had a few more sessions, but we never fell back into a weekly schedule. Charlotte, on the other hand, met with the Hospice support staff only once. The availability of professional help was appreciated, but we both opted to work things through on our own.

Charlotte and I had stayed away from Pacific Street for nearly six months, completely avoiding the old neighborhood. We heard that the restoration on the old house was complete and that Landlord Bill had found a new tenant. Life was beginning to resume. I needed to see for myself and, after all, the six-month anniversary was approaching.

With Charlie and Tanner joining me in the truck, I forced myself to drive those familiar San Luis Obispo streets on a warm June evening. Though not quite able to park directly in front of the house, I got close enough to see.

The work on the house appeared complete. Lights blazed in the windows. Furniture and boxes were stacked neatly on the front patio. I had heard a woman was moving in. Sitting there in the truck, I wondered who she was, what she might know about the fire. How does she feel about living in that house? I didn't want to intrude, but the living room light shining in our old house acted as a tempting beacon. Part of me just wanted to park the truck and walk inside, as if I could somehow pick up the pieces of the last six months and pretend everything was still OK.

There was a short, narrow hallway connecting the bathroom and two rear bedrooms in the old house. The hallway was lined with personal memorabilia, things that Charlotte and I supposedly thought were special. A framed newspaper article from when I won a local standup comedy contest, a handbill from Oxford University in 1976 when I participated in a campus debate and certificates of recognition given to Charlotte over the years.

During the fire, flames shot up from the basement directly on to that wall. Everything was destroyed. Nothing was left of our little personal shrine, no trace of our supposed accomplishments.

Sitting in the truck, thinking back over everything, the message wasn't lost on me. None of that stuff matters. *It never did, Dave, I reminded myself. Wipe all that from your mind. Focus on what really matters.* I am. I will. I promise.

My friend Leslie Halls, one of the first to contact us after the December fire, told me about grief markers. Her late husband Lee dropped dead of a heart attack at the age of forty-two. Leslie described the process of dealing with the passage of time. "You start marking even the smallest anniversaries of tragic events," she said. "One month. Six months. One year. Two years. There's no way to avoid it."

She's right. That's probably why I went to Pacific Street that night. With the six-month anniversary looming, I needed to see the lights burning once again in that old house. I wanted to know that the lemon tree that Charlotte and I planted together in the front yard continued to grow. Most importantly, I needed to know that life had returned, unafraid of any lingering ghosts.

A few minutes on Pacific Street seemed long enough. Time to return with my new dogs to my new home in Atascadero, where my new life was unfolding. I haven't returned to Pacific Street since.

They remain with us in the living room of our new home, tucked away safely behind glass on the upper shelf of a barrister bookcase. Triptych is on the far left. Tripper next to him, with that swatch of red bathrobe still draped over him. Trio lies in the center. Then Tess. Topper lies on the far right, his snazzy purple collar atop the cedar box.

Some favorite photographs in a small plastic case are propped up against the side wall.

Our new cats constantly eye the looming oak case with the intensity of Sir Edmund Hillary preparing to scale Mt. Everest, but they sense somehow to stay away. They understand that this shelf and the space above it are sacred ground. No cats allowed.

We've put the cremains in a bookcase in the living room simply because that's the safest place in a house bursting with such energetic animals. Also because we walk by that cabinet repeatedly every day, and we can make frequent quiet connections to our beloved companions. Sometimes we pause to say hello. Even if we say nothing, we're still thinking about them.

Charlotte and I haven't really discussed the question of what we will do eventually with the cremains. Bury them? Cart them off to some special place? Or just keep them with us, adding on as other pets die? We don't have the answer yet. There's no real hurry. Part of me, however, feels all five should remain together. That's how they died. That's how we remember them. All five together.

Talking with one of the volunteers at our county facility, I discovered what happens to the unwanted dogs and cats who are euthanized by San Luis Obispo County. Afterwards, the dead animal bodies are dumped and sealed in containers and shipped to Los Angeles, where they are cremated. Those cremains are then shipped to southeast Asia and sold as industrial fertilizer.

It's a consolation to us that Tess was spared that fate. She didn't die anonymously, only to become fertilizer in some foreign country. Because of us, Tess knew what it was like to have a home, to have a name and what it was like to be loved, albeit for only twenty-five days. But how do you shake "What Might Have Been?" We've tried to move beyond that stage. Given the alternative, we realize now that for one, brief, barking moment, Tess was actually a pretty lucky dog. And we were equally lucky to have found her.

Later that summer Charlotte approached me with her "serious face." She wanted to talk. "I don't want to do Christmas this year, OK?" Actually, it was more a statement than a question. I understood. "It's going to be tough enough as it is," Charlotte continued. "I don't want to do anything. No tree. No decorations. No gifts. No Christmas. Nothing. OK?"

My response was a long, knowing embrace. I felt relieved since I had been thinking the same thing for weeks, but there was a reluctance to bring the issue up given Charlotte's overwhelming fondness for the holiday.

So no Christmas in 1998. Nor in 1999. More grief markers. We'll know things are better when Christmas finally returns to our house.

San Luis Obispo County Telegram-Tribune   February 13, 1998

For Charlie, My Funny Valentine

He has long brown ears and the saddest eyes I've ever seen. He slobbers on everyone and everything. Constantly. He takes in more water than *Titanic*, inhaling the stuff by the gallon, somehow managing to get his ears soaked in the process.

He is always hungry and equally starved for attention; it is a personal insult if you ignore him for even a second. He thinks nothing of lunging up on the couch, or the bed, to join you. He can't tell the cat box from the icebox. His nose is in everything. He refuses to obey. Walk with him, and he's likely to trip you.

I swear that if you looked up the word "dumb" in the dictionary, you would find not only him, but his entire family.

Oh. I forgot about the gas. Big time.

The first two families he lived with (that should be a clue right there) called him Harley. I immediately changed that to Charlie, Charles Foster Kanine to

be precise, a basset hound who waddled into our lives last week with absolutely no intention of ever leaving.

A published study by psychologist Stanley Coren ranks the seventy-nine major breeds of dogs in terms of obedience and intelligence. The border collie came out number one. The basset hound trailed well behind at a less-than-respectable seventy-one, landing in the category of "Dogs Least Likely to Succeed as Watchdogs."

These are, according to Coren, "breeds that have been judged to be the most difficult. During initial training, these breeds may need thirty or forty repetitions before they show the first inkling that they have a clue as to what is expected of them." A second published profile of the basset hound suggests that Charlie will be both affectionate and difficult to housebreak. Guilty as charged.

I blame this situation totally, completely, on Charlotte. It was her idea to visit the Woods Humane Society Shelter. She just wanted to look, my wife insisted. The minute she left, I knew we were in trouble. More than an hour later, she was back, empty-handed and broken-hearted.

"They had the perfect dog out there, a basset hound," Charlotte reported. "He's so cute, David. But someone else already adopted him."

Thank you, I remember shouting to myself. A basset hound? Are we crazy? It was difficult enough to even consider getting a new dog so soon. A basset hound was the furthest thing from my canine wish list. Too stupid, I argued. Way too much trouble.

The point became moot. Harley was off with another family. Charlotte let the issue drop. I still remember the disappointment in her voice. One week later, Aleida Lund from Woods called. Harley was back—were we still interested?

Even the skeptic in me realized that this was some kind of sign. I reluctantly drove out to Woods with Charlotte, armed with a thousand reasons to say no. They all disappeared as Aleida guided us down the concrete runway to the last cage on the left. Harley, slobbering in excitement, pounced out of the cage and leaped into Charlotte's embrace with the greatest of ease. From that first moment, it was clear that these two were destined to be together. Charles Foster Kanine had finally found a home.

Our first week together has been wonderful. True, hardly a moment doesn't pass when I'm not shoving Charlie away. Perhaps you've seen us together at Laguna Lake or Heilmann Park—I'm the one doing the begging. All this will settle, in time. Stanley Coren is probably right about Charlie. He is definitely a slow-witted, underachieving, sad-eyed, always-thirsty, gas-emitting, drool of a dog. That will never change. But Coren was wrong about one thing.

This basset hound is a better retriever for Charlotte and me than any dog we've ever known. Finding and bringing back lost pieces of our hearts, one by one.

Good dog, Charlie. Good dog.

ELEVEN

Making Room For More

*A*ny lingering doubt I felt about the need for writing this book vanished on Wednesday, August 26, 1998.

My newspaper column had been appearing in the *San Luis Obispo County Telegram-Tribune* for five-and-a-half years, running on Tuesdays and Fridays. A general interest column, sometimes humorous, often personal, but always non-political. Pets and pet issues were a favorite topic from when I first introduced my readers to Topper and Triptych in February 1993. Periodically, I would write about people and organizations involved in the local humane movement. Our own pets often stepped into the spotlight. Yet in tracking the last 207 published columns, only 16 dealt specifically with pets. Hardly a crusade.

A new executive editor came to town in July 1998. The previous editor, John Moore, had left after the *Telegram-Tribune* was purchased by Knight Ridder earlier in the year. Hailing from Kentucky, Moore's replacement, Sandy Duerr, boasted an impressive journalism resume. She seemed sharp, accomplished, and determined to revamp our sleepy small-town daily paper.

After spending little more than a month in her new position, in a new community, Sandy called me into her office that Wednesday afternoon. With a manila folder bulging with old columns in her hand, she began discussing some "changes" she expected from my column.

No more pet columns in the newspaper. No more essays drawn from my personal life. Fire or no fire, Sandy simply wasn't interested in animals. Sitting across the round table from her, I became uncomfortable and tight-lipped as I listened to her surprising analysis of my work. This was not the meeting I expected.

She reached for one of my columns. "Here...you wrote this one about the kittens that were dumped on the side of the road. The mother and daughter found them...took them in. You wrote an open letter to whomever dumped the kittens." She paused, scanning the column again, then looking over at me innocently. "You really should have written about the mother and daughter instead and showed things from their perspective. It just sort of struck me as a missed opportunity, you know?"

Things went downhill from there. I couldn't understand why a new editor who hadn't even bothered to try and get to know me, was detailing everything that was wrong with my writing. Arguing would have been pointless. The meeting couldn't have ended soon enough.

She received my letter of resignation the next morning. In part, I wrote, "You tell me to stop writing about pets and pet issues. You might as well ask me to stop breathing."

Statistics indicate that more than 60 percent of all American households have at least one pet; a growing number have more than one. Still, there are millions of others, like Sandy Duerr, who just don't understand the extent of the human-animal companion bond and why it's such an important topic—especially for a newspaper. It was time to move on.

On the Friday of Labor Day weekend, I was again reminded that we don't choose animals; they choose us. My radio show always wraps up on Friday with a pet segment where we work with two local shelters and the county pound in trying to adopt out dogs and cats. I always try to make an extra effort whenever the county folks appear because they bring the "death row" dogs. The radio show is pretty much their last chance at public exposure. It's not fifteen minutes of fame, it's fifteen minutes of life.

That Friday, Stephanie Ruggerone, Animal Services Director, and one of her field officers came by. The officer seemed excited because her vacation started on Saturday, and Baja was calling. Dogs and cats are identified strictly by numbers at the county pound, but we try to give them a name on the radio show to improve chances of adoption. The dog that morning was christened Cabo in honor of the officer's upcoming vacation destination.

What a sad and sorrowful animal this was. Cabo appeared to be a sorry-stick-of-a-dog, little more than skin and bones. He was a tannish brown, shepherd-corgi mix, maybe seven months old. I was immediately struck by the fear in his eyes. He knew. He was a dead dog walking.

Cabo remained on the officer's lap the entire fifteen minutes, visibly shaking, staring straight ahead, cowering if anyone tried to speak directly to him. Physical and emotional abuse had obviously taken its toll. Now the clock was ticking. Cabo had until Monday before he would be put down.

I tried my best, enthusiastically talking the dog up to the listeners. Stephanie tried to emphasize how a little love can turn any dog around. We both knew this would be an uphill battle.

At the end of the segment, I walked around the console and squatted down next to Cabo, scratching softly behind his ear, trying to reassure him. He licked the back of my hand once. I didn't feel particularly good about Cabo's chances.

The dog haunted me for the rest of the day and into the night. I thought about Tess and how at least she didn't die unloved. No animal should be put down without knowing love, especially not one who had been so badly abused. I called around to friends.

"There's this dog…." The response was always the same. "Sorry, Dave, we'd like to, but…." Sure, I understood. Still, I kept trying. I didn't dare say a word to Charlotte, largely out of fear that she might try to have me committed for even *thinking* of another animal.

Sleep didn't come easy that night. I wrestled with the image of this scrawny dog glued to the officer's lap, too afraid to move. On Saturday morning, I made a point of sticking close to home, one eye on the clock. Around 11 p.m., I called Animal Services. "No, no visitors for Cabo," they reported.

The county pound is closed on Sunday. Monday would be too late. That meant something had to be done soon. I started verbalizing what my heart had been telling me for the past twenty-four hours. *This dog cannot be put down. Go get him, Dave. Go get him.*

I tried to appear casual and noncommittal as I searched out Charlotte, stretched out on the living room couch, her head buried in a mystery novel.

"Um, I thought I'd run down to Animal Services. That dog from yesterday is still there. I'm sort of concerned about his chances."

Charlotte didn't even bother looking up. "OK."

"I thought maybe I'd sign him out and try and get him a foster home."

"OK."

"Charlotte, I'm not looking for another dog. Really. We'll just foster him. That's all."

My wife finally looked at me. "That's fine, David. Go get the dog."

Within the hour, I was kneeling down on the cold, damp cement slab of Cabo's cramped cage, clutching his paperwork, trying my best to make a love connection. His food in the nearby bowl hadn't been touched. If I spoke too loudly, he responded by peeing. Other anxious dogs, no doubt envious, barked and barked in nearby cages, trying to get some attention.

Cabo kept his distance from me, still very much afraid and uncertain, the loud barking only making him more unsettled. I calmly extended the back of my hand. He licked it once. He knew.

"It's going to be OK, pal," I whispered, rubbing my hand gently over his silky smooth coat. "Everything is going to be fine."

One of the animal control officers walked by, clearly surprised to see someone in Cabo's cage. "Good thing you're here," she said. "That dog wasn't going to make it otherwise."

When I took the dog home, two changes were immediate. First, Charlotte changed his name from Cabo to Simon. And second, within forty-eight hours our new dog's status shifted from foster to permanent.

New count: Three cats. Three dogs. Four kittens.

One of the positive results of moving to Atascadero was Charlotte's increased involvement in the North County Humane Society. They are good people doing a tough job. Charlotte was invited to join the shelter's board of directors and she eagerly accepted.

Each week Charlotte dropped off a bag of cat food or a bundle of paper towels at the shelter. Sometimes I went with her. Most times I tried to stay away—too tempting. During the kitten season, the shelter is known to overflow with cats, typically more than one hundred on any given day. It's tough to walk inside and come out empty-handed.

We stopped by on a Saturday afternoon in late October. I followed Charlotte inside, minding my own business. Leaning across the counter, I started chatting with a staff member when suddenly I felt a pair of sharp claws dig into my left shoulder.

"What the…" I yelled.

I looked around and came face-to-face with my tormenter, a runt of a gray-and-white kitten. Easily bored within seconds, she moved on, next jumping over to Charlotte, and then on to the counter to check out the volunteers.

We never choose pets. They always choose us.

The staff immediately started chatting up the kitten, Dorthea, who had been born four months ago and abandoned by the side of a road in Atascadero. Already spayed, Dorthea would always be small, but definitely high energy. Clearly an interesting kitty, but neither Charlotte nor I felt ready to commit. We left the shelter empty-handed.

Yet, for the rest of the day, our routine conversation kept returning to Dorthea. She had definitely made an impression on us. There was something in Charlotte's voice when she talked about her. Still, there were already three dogs and seven cats occupying the house. Some of our friends might have worried about us adopting so many pets, so quickly, but we didn't care.

Charlotte and I discussed the issue at length. After the fire, we were immediately surrounded by a wave of friends and strangers who made all the difference. We couldn't have survived without that support. Yet, as the initial shock subsided, people tended to retreat, understandably shifting back into their own lives and needs. Charlotte and I found ourselves on our own more and more.

Each household must decide their comfort zone with pets. I know so many people who can only handle one or two. That's fine. With us, a new standard evolved. In our house, Charlotte and I never wanted to be more than an arm's length from a dog or a cat. We were using them, I guess, to create this huge, furry, four-legged security blanket around us. In the process we created a new pet owner mindset of "lose five pets, go save ten."

There was definitely that initial urge to find new pets, to go on some kind of adoption binge, but Charlotte and I never lowered our standards. We said no, as often as we said yes, to potential adoptees. There was a challenging transition period as we integrated all these animals from diverse backgrounds together.

All the new animals get along and there is a blessed spirit of détente throughout the house. In fact, bringing a third dog home actually turned out to be quite a masterful stroke. With Simon, Tanner now has a friendly rival who can run by his side, race him to squirrel holes, and wrestle in the grass. When we're at the park, Charlie stays on the leash, while Tanner and Simon take off and play together. It works out pretty well.

Whatever small happiness we found in 1998 came largely from this new four-legged family. A sense of love and calm filters through all the rooms. No more lonely mornings. Charlotte has discovered what it's like to wake up at 6 a.m. and find herself covered with all seven cats demanding to be fed.

Which brings us back to little Dorthea. She had definitely made an impression on us with her spunky, outgoing style. Her name kept coming up in conversation, a signal that some connection had definitely been made. That night, we decided to go back on Sunday and adopt her. Charlotte floated out the door the next afternoon, cat carrier in hand. She seemed genuinely excited. Within the hour she returned, empty-handed, quiet and subdued.

Someone else had adopted Dorthea after we left, Charlotte explained in a rather glum voice. I tried to console her, hiding any disappointment and pretending that it wasn't that big of a deal. "We have enough cats already," Charlotte sighed.

"Yeah," I lied, in agreement. "The last thing we need is another cat. She's in a good home, that's what counts." And we said it with enough sincerity to almost believe ourselves.

So we went back to enjoying the animals we had, trying to shake the thought of little Dorthea from our minds. But Sunday became Monday, which then became Tuesday, and we were still thinking of that little gray-and-white dynamo who liked to fly around and land in people's hearts. We couldn't help but beat up on ourselves for failing to seize the moment.

Wednesday afternoon, Wendy called from the shelter. "Good news," she chirped over the phone. "The woman decided not to keep Dorthea after all. Need another cat?"

Need one? No. Want one? Want Dorthea? Absolutely! She joined us within the hour, and we named her Eudora. Hannah and Eudora bonded with one another immediately, becoming inseparable playmates.

New count: Three cats. Three dogs. Five kittens.

San Luis Obispo County Telegram-Tribune   July 28, 1998

A Letter To A Stranger

Usually I write for many. This time I focus on only one.

You know who you are. I suspect you live somewhere around Atascadero. You own a female cat. She was never spayed. Maybe you meant to. Or you didn't have the money. Or you don't believe in spaying cats. Or you just don't understand the big picture about cat overpopulation.

It doesn't matter now. But your female cat became pregnant—again?—because that's what happens to female cats who aren't spayed. And sometime in May, that cat gave birth to a litter of at least five kittens.

That must have complicated things. You didn't want these kittens. Too many. Too much of a hassle. All that sneezing bothered you. They were sick. They had to go. Sure, I don't blame you. It happens all the time.

So what did you do? Try to give them away to friends? Take out a newspaper ad? Show them off at a local Farmers' Market?

Call your vet? Spend $40 and let the North County Humane Society take them in?

Did you even consider for a moment about possibly keeping one or two of them? Or was it your first choice to just stuff all five squealing kittens in a cardboard box and dump them along side of the road in the wee hours of Thursday, June 25?

Was there any hesitation on your part? Any guilt? Did you leave them any food? Did you look in your rearview mirror as you sped away, or did you just stare straight ahead? Were you ever tempted to turn around, even for a second? Don't worry, nobody saw you. Or if they did, they simply kept driving, guilty as you.

Not that you care, but you should know that one kitten died within hours, hit by a car. And that a second kitten fled into the field, left to survive on his or her own at six weeks old.

That left only three. That's how many a concerned mother and daughter were able to rescue when they stopped their car that morning. Lucky for those surviving three, the mother headed directly for her vet. Of course, you could have made that same drive, but that's all academic at this point, isn't it?

I do have some good news. All three surviving kittens were adopted into warm and loving homes through the North County Humane Society. Do you remember that small black sliver of fur with the white specks? The female who was probably always sneezing around you? Well, she's ours now.

Her right eye is gone thanks to a severe infection and whatever else she was exposed to during those first six weeks. Dr. Knighton cleaned out what was left of that eye and sewed it shut. The sutures came out last Saturday. The infection finally went away. Her fur is starting to grow back. Despite what you did, this kitten has bounced back nicely.

We named her Hannah, our little ray of hope. I wish you could have seen her last night, curled up on the pillow next to Charlotte, quietly purring herself to sleep. The image of those two sleeping together, seeing this new bond form, is almost enough to wipe away the more painful images of late. Tell me, how have you been sleeping lately? Any bad dreams?

I guess we have you to thank for Hannah. What a great cat she's going to be. Yet our appreciation is tempered by the callousness, the desperation, of someone who would simply toss her out like garbage. It would be easier to accept all this had you been an isolated case. Unfortunately, according to my animal rescue friends, you're not.

So, one last question for you. How many more Hannahs will it take before you finally have your cat fixed? At least now I understand why cats need nine lives.

But when I see what Hannah went through, I wonder if nine lives are enough.

TWELVE

Searching For Simon

*T*here must be a law, postulate, axiom, policy, rule, commandment, directive, whatever. Something that somehow, somewhere, in some way, makes it clear that in any one twelve-month period, only one traumatic incident per family is allowed. No exceptions, please.

I always assumed that to be the case, at least up until late in the afternoon on Sunday, November 8, 1998. Then reality came knocking once again, introducing us to a whole different dimension of pet loss.

That Sunday was a lazy fall afternoon; nothing much on our schedule. We had just bought a new car for Charlotte, a Honda CRV. She was long overdue for this, and now with Simon, our small Mitsubishi needed replacing. We decided to load up Tanner, Charlie, and Simon and cruise down to Pismo Beach for lunch at the county's only Greek restaurant. Afterwards, we swung over to Arroyo Grande to visit some friends and let the dogs run.

Heading home to Atascadero on Highway 101, everything seemed routine. Charlotte drove while I stretched out in the passenger seat. Charlie, Tanner, and Simon were sacked out in the back.

Highway 101 winds and twists through the Los Padres National Forest for about seven miles before reaching the summit of the Cuesta

Grade at 1,522 feet. From there, the two northbound lanes dip down and begin a gradual curve towards the exit for Santa Margarita, a small rural blip of about 1,200 people. We made it over the grade safely, but after that, everything else is hazy.

According to the California Highway Patrol (CHP) accident report, Charlotte was driving in the left lane, and suddenly, unexpectedly, drifted over to the right, directly in front of another car. Then she swerved back, over-correcting in the process. Our car continued swerving. Based on the CHP report, we proceeded to flip once, flip twice, and slide on our left side for about two hundred yards before slamming roof-first into a towering oak tree in the center divider. The impact with the tree was so strong that it forced us upright again, facing the opposite direction.

I remember careening down the highway. And yelling—that kind of heart-in-your-throat, oh-my-god panic scream normally heard on speeding roller coasters. I honestly thought we were going to die. Thankfully, we were wearing our safety harnesses. Only when the car came to a complete halt did I accept the fact that we would live.

Instinctively I turned towards Charlotte. Her face seemed horribly bruised, all black and blue. She was talking rapidly, incoherently—fragments of sentences shooting out, most of it babble, but she seemed to be asking repeatedly what had happened. Charlotte was alive and that was all that mattered at the moment. The engine was still running, so I reached over and turned off the ignition, fearful of some type of gas explosion.

Then I twisted with some difficulty to look over my shoulder into the back compartment. For the second time in twelve months, that queasy knot in my stomach returned. The rear window of the vehicle had busted out completely.

All three dogs were missing.

Like the night of the fire, a surrealistic haze returned. I lost all sense of time and space. A thousand different emotions pulled me in a thousand different directions. How quickly everything can change within seconds. One minute, we were riding along quietly, then all hell broke loose.

The back of my left hand was covered with tiny cuts, most likely from flying pieces of glass. My right side felt very sore. Overall, I felt light-headed and more than a little disoriented.

My crumpled passenger door wouldn't open, so I pulled myself out through the window and stumbled around the rear of the car. No sign of the dogs. I had half-expected to see three bodies. After all, they had gone through this same skid and tumbling unrestrained.

Other drivers immediately stopped and a wave of concerned people quickly surrounded us. Out of the corner of my eye, I spotted Charlie across the road, a woman hanging on to him tightly. "Thank you," I mumbled to myself. No sign of Tanner or Simon. They would have to wait.

My focus returned to Charlotte as I made my way toward her window, also broken out in the accident. She clearly took the brunt of the collision; her bruised face must have smashed against the steering wheel.

"David, David, what happened? What happened?" she kept repeating.

"Charlotte, are you OK? Are you OK?"

"What happened? What happened?" was all she could say. I had no answers.

A physician was one of the first people to reach Charlotte, so I backed away. Everyone encouraged me to sit down, but I couldn't. For the next ten minutes, I, too, babbled and frantically pleaded with person after person to please find my missing dogs.

"I have to find my dogs! You don't understand, I've already lost five pets! I can't lose two more. Please?!"

You're barking at the moon, Dave, my heart answered. This was a major interstate highway, quickly becoming a traffic nightmare. The priorities became rapidly clear: Charlotte. Me. Traffic. No one was going to worry about two lost dogs at this point.

Paramedics arrived and calmly escorted me to the ambulance, insisting that I lie down, patiently ignoring my anguished diatribe about missing dogs. They warned me that I risked being paralyzed. It took twenty minutes to remove Charlotte from what was left of our car. They placed us on stretchers in the ambulance and started IVs. Meanwhile, an extremely helpful sheriff's deputy snagged Charlie and stashed the basset hound in her patrol car.

The priority became getting us down the grade to Sierra Vista Medical Center. Still no word about Simon and Tanner. Eyewitnesses reported that all three dogs bolted across the two northbound lanes. Charlie was safe, but Simon and Tanner, obviously spooked and in a panic, must have made a beeline for the woods. Santa Margarita, the closest town, was at least two miles away. Between here and there were acres of rugged, tree-dense terrain. My dogs had disappeared into a giant black hole. And we were speeding away in the opposite direction, once again helpless to rescue those whom we loved the most.

They kept us in the emergency room for five hours, mostly doing tests and X-rays. Because I had been asleep at the beginning of the accident, and in such a relaxed state, my injuries were minor. A cut hand, a few cracked ribs and a mild concussion.

Charlotte wasn't as lucky. She banged up her right kneecap and there was concern about a possible fracture in her left wrist. Her right cheek was cut and her face looked puffy and bruised. She complained about dizziness. To this day, Charlotte has no recall of the accident. There's about a fifteen-minute gap in her memory; quite common, we're told, for traffic accident victims.

Lying in the emergency room, I couldn't avoid flashbacks to the previous December. We were back in the same hospital, in the same emergency room. Dr. Sainsbury, who had treated us the night of the fire, was even on duty down the hall, busy with other patients. Several of the staff recognized us, remembering the fire and our earlier trauma. They kept asking about our new dogs. I had no answers.

Our good friends David and Karen Gray were notified of our

accident, and they showed up immediately. An hour later, KVEC station owner Frank Sheahan appeared unexpectedly in the emergency room. Frank, the avid dog lover, had been with us through the dark days after the fire. Here he was, once again, without waiting to be asked.

Around 8 p.m., a CHP report came through announcing that a dog matching Tanner's description had been spotted in some underbrush near the top of the grade. Attempts had been made to coax the dog out, but he wouldn't budge. Still anxious, I wanted to go see for myself, but the staff wasn't ready to release us. Frank volunteered to drive up and see what he could find. We agreed to rendezvous as soon as possible.

Only one dog had been spotted. That didn't bode well, I thought. Simon and Tanner always ran together. How could they have separated? Still feeling dizzy and drained and more than a little anxious, Charlotte and I were released shortly after 9 p.m. David and Karen bundled us into their car, and off we went.

We found Frank parked on the shoulder of the southbound lanes, just across from our accident scene. Southbound lanes? That meant one of the dogs had initially crossed over two lanes of northbound traffic, and then doubled back across four lanes to the other side of the highway. Our anxiety level increased with this realization. Even worse, Frank hadn't seen anything during the last hour. David and Karen drove Charlotte home while Frank and I continued to search in the dark with flashlights. We called repeatedly for Simon and Tanner, wandering off the road, over a creek, into a nearby pasture in total darkness. No sign of the dogs. How far had these guys gone? Which side of the highway were they on? The answer would have to wait until morning.

Monday, at sunrise, I dragged myself out of bed. Moving slowly, I felt rather light-headed, but nothing was about to keep me away from the accident scene. Back on the highway, I could see that to the right of the highway, directly across from the accident scene, are railroad tracks that quickly veer off, heading into Santa Margarita.

There's also a private dirt road leading back into the hills, and a solitary house. On the left side of the highway, another road cuts due west, towards a string of scattered homes. The dogs could be anywhere. I didn't know where to begin.

Dieter Nicklesberg, loyal friend as always, drove up from San Luis Obispo to help. He searched the right side of the highway while I retraced the previous night's journey on the other side. Unfortunately, daylight wasn't enough. There was still no sign. The morning rush hour traffic roared past me. I kept shuddering at the thought of Tanner and Simon trying to cross this busy highway.

Around 7:30, I crossed back over, south of the accident, working my way back up along the shoulder of the northbound lanes. The private dirt road was parallel to me, separated by what was left of a rusty chain link fence.

From off to the right, I heard the toot of a horn. A white pickup truck was heading down the dirt road towards the highway. The man at the wheel waved for me to meet him at the gate. This had to be good news.

Yelling out for Dieter, I ran, trying not to trip in my excitement. It had only taken an hour. I couldn't believe our good fortune. The man turned out to be the owner of that solitary house by the highway. I only half-heard his explanation through my excitement. My concentration zeroed in on the back seat of the truck cab.

There sat Tanner, smiling and healthy, tail wagging, glad to see me. But Tanner was alone. Poor Simon was still missing.

Simon's mysterious disappearance introduced Charlotte and me to a completely different form of pet loss. Despite the horrific tragedy involving Topper, Triptych, Tripper, Trio, and Tess, we had one overwhelming and gratifying consolation. We knew what happened. We saw their bodies. We had closure.

But this was different. There was no sign of Simon. Where was he? What happened to him? Was he still alive, capable of surviving on his own? Charlotte and I had to struggle with the thought that we might never see Simon again, not really know what happened to him. I never thought anything could match the anxiety of the fire—it took less than a year for me to learn otherwise.

And we worried especially because it was Simon. He was still shy and tentative, peeing in response to almost any command, a mere wisp of bones and skin. Tanner was smart. Charlie was strong. But Simon? Out there on his own in the freezing cold of night? He hadn't been with us that long. How could he possibly find us? How could he understand about the accident? Charlotte and I didn't sleep much that week. This time, there were no sedatives to help us.

The *Telegram-Tribune* carried a story about our accident and photos of Simon and Tanner, which helped spread the word. In the days that followed, we heard from dog and cat owners alike, all telling incredible tales about survival. Dogs and cats, missing for days, weeks, months, then suddenly, miraculously returning home. Hang tough, Dave and Charlotte, they urged. Simon will appear.

The lingering guilt I felt about the fire took on a new dimension that week. We couldn't do anything about December. However, I wasn't about to give up on Simon without a fight.

The first thing I did, following the advice of friends, was to visualize repeatedly the image of Simon coming home. Think it, and he will come. Over and over again, I replayed that scene. *Here comes Simon. He's coming home.*

Studying the area surrounding the accident, we concluded that Simon likely headed towards Santa Margarita, the only town in close proximity. Following the railroad tracks from where the accident happened would have brought Simon directly into town where he could forage at night.

As before, our concerned friends came out. On Tuesday morning, nine friends blanketed Santa Margarita with fliers. Simon's photo appeared everywhere. A reward was offered. We even stopped people on the street, asking if they had seen our lost dog.

More phone calls came in, all reporting sightings. Simon was seen up in Templeton, fifteen miles to the north; down in Santa Maria, forty-five minutes to the south. On the west side of Atascadero. On the east side of Atascadero. This guy had more sightings than Elvis.

The toughest call came from the CHP. They had the dead body of a brown dog lying on the entrance ramp to Highway 101 in Paso Robles, north of Templeton. Could Simon have run that far? I drove for fifteen gut-wrenching minutes because I had to know. When I first came upon the body, lifeless on the side of the road, I slumped forward in my car. From a distance, he looked just like Simon.

Except for that green collar. Simon wore a red collar. Wrong dog. Thank you. Thank you.

We had seven other false alarms that week, where either Charlotte or I drove out to where a brown dog had been spotted. A pattern emerged over Wednesday, Thursday and Friday. Each day, I would just cruise around in my truck, picking different neighborhoods. In the afternoon, Tanner and I would wander the open country roads around Templeton. At night, we'd swing down through Santa Margarita, slowly driving the dirt alleys between houses, hoping to catch a glimpse, or hear a familiar bark.

I wasn't ashamed to pray, not afraid to beg. Please, please let me find this dog. He's only been with us for two months. We've already lost five. You owe me one. You owe me at least one.

The image of Simon coming home safe remained fixed in my mind, but his chances grew slimmer with each passing day. By the weekend, Simon had been gone for six full days and seven long nights. Charlotte and I felt so empty. We could replace the car, but we couldn't replace Simon.

"Look, we've done just about everything we can," I finally told Charlotte on Saturday, after our umpteenth search. "Simon has got to emerge somewhere. We can't find him if he doesn't want to be found."

"I know," Charlotte agreed, still harboring pain from the accident. "I'm just so worried about him."

Me too. Tanner and I continued our regular rounds of Templeton and Santa Margarita. Nothing on Saturday. Nothing on Sunday. Our friends continued to help. Cheri Lucas of the Second Chance at Love Humane Society spent an entire morning plodding through open pasture with a search dog, hoping somehow to pick up Simon's scent. Still nothing. Simon had been missing for an entire week, creating a chasm of sadness in our hearts.

Monday morning, November 16, barely 7:30 a.m. Eight days and counting. I stumbled out of bed after another night of tossing and turning caused by a mixture of back pain and anxiety. Despite all the animals, the house seemed exceptionally quiet and still that morning. I sat down at our breakfast bar, half-heartedly thumbing through the morning paper. The phone rang. It was Valerie Johnson from the radio station.

"There's a woman who just called from Santa Margarita. She has a stray dog in her backyard."

Charlotte, sitting on the living room couch with Hannah, leaned forward, suddenly curious, sensing along with me that this was important. "This could be it!" I yelled over my shoulder, anxiously punching the keypad to call Santa Margarita.

The woman's name was Cindy Warren. Her house was in the southwest corner of town, the section closest to the accident. Cindy heard a stray dog barking Sunday night, but it was too dark to see anything. "Yes, he's in the backyard right now, huddled behind the wood pile," Cindy reported. Yes, brown. Yes, a red collar. Yes, very shy. Yes, she'll wait for us to drive down.

Yes. Yes. Yes. Yes. YES!

"Let's go!" I shouted, slamming down the phone. "This has got to be him."

Charlotte and I flew to Santa Margarita via Toyota Airlines. The drive took only a matter of minutes, but even in our speed, it seemed an eternity. We felt excited, anxious, confused—perhaps too confused, because we quickly became lost in Santa Margarita, trying to figure out exactly which house on "I" Street belonged to Cindy.

Frustrated and starting to reach for the cell phone, I spotted a woman standing alone in her driveway. Dropping the phone, I pressed harder on the gas pedal.

Already late for work, Cindy didn't care about time. She had seen the flier and Simon's photo. An animal lover, Cindy wouldn't leave for work without knowing for sure. For her, there wasn't any doubt. Her four-legged guest out back had to be Simon.

We approached the backyard with some caution. Even if this was Simon, we had to be careful. I didn't want him to panic and bolt away again. Cindy quietly pointed to the far right corner, between a large brown wooden shed and a barbed wire fence. "Back there," she said. "He's been there all night."

I couldn't see a thing. Squinting, I looked again. There, just behind the woodpile, was a speck of brown, barely visible.

"Simon?" I called gently, trying my best to remain calm.

No response. One more time. "Simon…Simon?"

Slight movement behind the wood pile. I took a breath. And then we saw him emerge. Simon, *our* Simon, thin to the bone, walking ever so cautiously. Hesitating, wanting to see us, but also very afraid. He gingerly took a few steps and paused. The uncertainty in his eyes was obvious.

Charlotte and I both immediately squatted down, opening our arms, trying to encourage and reassure Simon from a distance. "C'mon, Simon. Good dog. C'mon, boy."

His tail started wagging. He came closer, still cautious. Simon's feet seemed to hurt. We kept calling him. "That's a good dog. C'mon, Simon. C'mon, boy."

The message finally connected. With his hips swaying as he walked, Simon slowly approached us. He knew how happy we were.

"C'mon, Simon. C'mon, boy."

Closer and closer he edged, our arms outstretched to welcome him. He responded with repeated licks of recognition as Charlotte and I wrapped ourselves around him, smothering his dirty, smelly, tick-ridden, wonderful body.

Only then could we see the reason for Simon's painful walk. The pads on all four paws had been ripped to shreds from days of constant running. We would help them heal in time, but first we had to take our dog home.

Charlotte and I didn't say much to each other on the short drive back to Atascadero. We were both too busy fawning over Simon as he sat happily on Charlotte's lap, excitedly licking her face. She didn't mind as her arms lovingly locked around the dog, refusing to let go.

Looking back on the grueling events of those eight days, I think that's why we had such a happy ending this time. We refused to let go of Simon.

San Luis Obispo County Telegram-Tribune   *April 7, 1998*

When One Is Greater Than Two

Two is always greater than one. Always. Basic mathematical principle drilled into me since childhood. Apples. Kisses. Dollars. World Series baseball tickets. It doesn't matter. Having two is always better than one.

Yet, I've been rethinking my math lately, especially since we brought two dogs home to Atascadero. Charles Foster Kanine and Tanner have been with us since early February. Two dogs. Two months. Too much, I sometimes wonder out loud, as I watch (and listen) to this overly dynamic duo bounce around the house, playing some strange combination of canine ice hockey and rugby. What were we thinking when we decided on a pair of new dogs?

And I gaze forlornly at the solitary photograph hanging in our foyer. When I see Topper's familiar gaze, I remember. Two is not always greater than one. Especially not the one in this case.

Charlie the basset hound certainly tries. My, how he does try. After two months together, I can safely report this: a basset hound is not a dog. He's a four-legged teddy bear, in constant need of a hug. From the moment I wake up in the morning, to the moment I fall asleep at night, I apparently have one overriding mission in life—hug Charlie. That's it.

He follows me constantly throughout the house, like some type of celebrity stalker. If I sit, he sits; usually by pouncing on my lap. If I spend more than ten minutes on the computer, he waltzes over and nudges underneath my right arm with his snout. Time for a hug, Dave. Hug me, please. Hug me, or I'll drool all over your computer. I swear this dog was Rudolph Valentino in a previous life.

Driving anywhere with Charlie is impossible. Most dogs jump up inside the truck automatically. Not Charlie. No, he has to run around the outside of the truck one-two-three times first, no doubt performing some ancient basset ritual that protects him from my erratic driving. Even when we're both inside the cab, I still can't budge because Charlie has nuzzled up next to me—you guessed it—wanting another big hug.

Tanner, the young brown-and-white mixed breed, tries too. I call him Good Will Tanner after that Robin Williams movie about the troubled kid who's also a math genius. That's Tanner. Fastest dog I've ever seen. Smart as Albert Einstein. Snags a tennis ball in his mouth with the grace of Willie Mays.

But he's trouble, through and through. Gets into fights. Barks up a storm. Easily becomes jealous. Tough-guy attitude. A cigarette should be dangling out of his mouth instead of a chewstick. This dog would be Jimmy Cagney in a previous life—"You, you dirty cat."

I've read accounts over the years where people who experienced sudden loss immediately went out and remarried or began other new intense relationships. Sometimes it works; often times it doesn't. The situation is never easy because the new folks are always dealing with that memory, unfairly being compared to what came before.

As it has been with Charlie and Tanner. They're both good dogs. Such very good dogs. We're lucky and grateful to have them. But that wasn't enough for me initially. I've been distant, overly strict, far too demanding; punishing these new companions for something they had no control over, something that happened even before they ever came along.

That attitude changed early last week. I'm unable to pinpoint the exact moment of my epiphany, but this I know and finally accept. Charlie and Tanner are about as far away from Topper as the moon. That will always be. We're about to spend the next decade or so together with me donning a variety of hats: trainer, referee, coach, teacher, medic, guardian. Progress will be slow, but, hopefully, steady.

There are continued moments of melancholy around Topper's photo in the foyer, but Charlie and Tanner are slowly forcing me to recalculate my math. After all, they're not trying to prove that two is always greater than one. Just not less than. Equal. That's all, Dave. Equal.

THIRTEEN

T Is For Love

*E*motional storm clouds began forming in early November 1998 with both of us going through an automatic mental countdown to the December anniversary date. The car accident and the intense anxiety surrounding our search for Tanner and especially for Simon had worn us down even more. The first anniversary marker, we worried, could be the knockout punch.

So little was actually discussed about the impending anniversary. Charlotte and I both understood what was approaching, yet we had no idea of what we would do. On the one hand, there was no way we were going to leave the house on December 14. Yet the thought of being by ourselves was very unsettling. There had to be a compromise.

The anniversary fell on a Monday, but our anxiety stemmed more from thinking about that Sunday night. We decided to host an open house that Sunday, allowing us to stay home with our new menagerie while also being among close friends. The night would be simple and upbeat. Cookies and hot cider for everyone.

As promised, there were no signs of Christmas in our house that December, save for the smattering of holiday cards taped above the breakfast bar. What few holiday ornaments survived the fire remained neatly packed away in the garage, waiting for better days. Such starkness in December seemed foreign to me. I have always celebrated the holidays. But not this time around.

Our kind and supportive friends once again turned out, thankfully in shifts. Some came early and others waited to that last hour before arriving. Charlie, Tanner and Simon, overwhelmed by so many guests, stayed surprisingly quiet, observing everything from various corners of the living room. The eight cats stayed isolated in a rear bedroom, happy to stay away from people and noise.

The evening flew by. Little flashes regularly popped into my mind, taking me back one year, but I refused to stay there, zipping right back to the present. A day doesn't pass when I'm not haunted by images of the fire, but I don't allow them to linger too long. Everyone kept the conversation cheerful throughout the evening, with little direct mention of the five Ts. They were in the living room with us. No one really needed a reminder about why we had gathered.

The last few guests left shortly before 11 p.m. Charlotte and I collapsed on the couch, surrounded by our new wave of cats and dogs. *Hey, look, we made it,* I thought. We felt OK—more than OK—a huge sense of relief for getting through the critical first anniversary.

Some believe that the first year after a tragedy is the most difficult. We can certainly attest to that. Ingrid Pires had been so prophetic on my radio show when she warned how those first twelve months would be such a roller coaster. However, based on what others have shared with us, it's also not uncommon to experience major traumatic flashbacks years after an incident. One year later, this is all I can say: I feel pain daily. I try not to let that pain control me, yet I acknowledge it. That's as good as it gets.

That tear-soaked night in March when we stayed home from the Academy Awards party now seems light years away. I tell myself that I've made great strides since then. The tears still appear, though not as frequently.

Part of the process has been to learn how to hide intense pain behind a broad smile, to privatize my grief. People, even good friends, seem to assume that everything is fine because I'm back to cracking jokes. A classic case of laughing on the outside, crying on the inside. There remains an appreciation of life, but there's something different about me now. A twinkle, a certain innocence, is never coming back. There are days when I just go through the motions and other days when getting out of bed seems impossible. I haven't stopped living. I simply live differently.

Our priorities, meanwhile, changed drastically over the year. That anniversary trip to Tahiti, once in the planning stage, has been put on hold indefinitely. I can't remember the last time I spent serious money on clothes. Our book and CD collection probably won't ever be as extensive as before. The desire for nonessential material goods has waned.

Charlotte is blessed with beautiful, long, brown hair. The gray started creeping in a few years ago. Like many baby boomers, Charlotte opted at a certain point to add a little color to her life. No big deal.

Yet after the fire, I began to notice a change. Charlotte would go off to her hair appointment and later return with the gray untouched. More and more streaks of gray began to appear over time. I never mentioned that I noticed; however, one morning Charlotte announced matter-of-factly, "I'm doing this because of the fire. This is me. This is who I am now."

Meanwhile, the scars on my hands and wrists remain from the cuts I suffered breaking out the dining room windows during the fire. I guess I assumed that they would disappear over time. They haven't. For the rest of my life, I'll have these six tiny reminders of what happened.

I think of Charlotte and her gray hair. "This is me. This is who I am now."

And though we have to continue to work, Charlotte and I find a little less magic in our jobs. We linger around the house longer each morning, taking our time to leave. Charlotte brings work home much less often.

The fear of another fire has kept us pretty close to home. The thought of some exotic, getaway vacation was completely out of the question, despite the encouragement of well-meaning friends. Vacations were sparse and simple. We took only one trip together that first year, a short anniversary visit to Catalina Island in May. Charlotte also went home to Indianapolis to see her family and I made two weekend trips north to Seattle to visit my parents. We felt too uncomfortable about the prospect of leaving our new animals alone. One of us always had to be close to home.

There was also a tendency to avoid going out at all on Sunday nights. It just became an established rule—never on Sundays. When we did venture out at night, the regimen stayed the same. Don't go too far. Don't stay out too late. Don't drink too much, if at all. I would still get nervous and edgy if we were away from home for more than four hours. More often than not, at least one of the dogs came with us and waited in the car. Or, sometimes, only one of us went out, leaving the other at home to watch over things. We've even hired people to come in and sit with our animals. But mostly, we stayed home. Our friends understood.

On those rare excursions out, there's always an uneasy quiet on the trip home, particularly during the last few minutes as we ease off Highway 101 and cover the last mile to the house. It takes two quick turns on our new street in Atascadero to actually see the house. Neither Charlotte nor I mention it. We don't have to. We know what the other is thinking.

We look for the lights and the occasional cat in the front window. Only when we know that there's no sign of trouble does the anxiety and uneasiness disappear.

Until the next time.

Eventually I achieved a small victory with some of my family members. On a later trip to Los Angeles, once things were more settled, we stopped to visit my brother and sister-in-law, Bob and Anne. The visit went much smoother this time, a throwback to the old days. During our time together, Anne handed Charlotte two small, brightly wrapped gifts. "Here," she told Charlotte. "It's just a little something I picked up. I thought you might like them."

Two small picture frames emerged from the wrapping—one decorated around the border with dogs, the other with cats. In all the years with Topper, Bob and Anne had never given me any pet-related presents. This was clearly a first. A gesture that, perhaps, they too felt bad about Christmas, and were at least trying to understand. Too bad my brother is still allergic to animals.

Topper continues to go everywhere with me, still. Our daily dialogue continues, however one-sided. When I talk about him in public today, I make no apologies for the sense of loss I feel. Only in his passing do I appreciate the true impact of our relationship. Topper is the great love of my life, just as Triptych is the great love of Charlotte's life. I used to tell Topper repeatedly, usually while scratching his stomach for the umpteenth time: "There never has been, there never will be, a better dog."

Deep love. Great loss. Slow comeback. Uncertain future. That's the basic storyline. Make no mistake about it—an hour doesn't pass that Charlotte and I don't smile at least once because of the antics of our new crew. They're wonderful, all of them: Charlie, Tanner, Simon, Earl Grey, Tristan, Emma, Reuben, Romeo, Hannah, Alexander, and Eudora. They remind us why we first opened our hearts so long ago. These new pets make us happy—or at least, happier. In truth, they are our lifesavers, pulling Charlotte and me through the last twelve months.

People have sent us dozens of poems, articles, and quotations about animals since the fire. One of my favorites is this anonymous tribute, "He is your friend, your partner, your defender, your dog. You are his life, his love, his leader. He will be yours, faithful and true, to the last beat of his heart. You owe it to him to be worthy of such devotion."

These words best capture everything I had with Topper during fourteen wonderful years and everything I hoped to have with Tess. A sense of obligation to their memory lingers, for Triptych, Tripper, and Trio, as well. Some might think this is about guilt, while others would confuse it with grief. I prefer to explain my feelings as everlasting love.

So when the organizers of an animal conference in San Luis Obispo invited me to be the keynote speaker in March 1999, I didn't hesitate. Standing calmly before a room full of fellow animal lovers, I spoke of everlasting love and what Charlotte and I had learned in the aftermath of our loss. "Don't ever apologize for the grief you feel over the loss of an animal," I urged. "Don't let anyone try to minimize or question the emptiness you feel in your heart."

In closing, I described Topper, Triptych, Tripper, Trio, and Tess as five animal companions who left us far too soon, but in many ways, they would never leave us. They made an indelible impact on our lives and I offered a public pledge to the memory of three special cats and two extraordinary dogs:

> We will remember that they enriched our lives from the very first moment. They never gave us any reason to regret opening our home and our hearts to animal companions.
>
> We will be grateful for the time, however brief, we were able to spend together. We enjoyed every touch, every nuzzle. We never regretted missing a social event or cutting short a vacation to be home and spend more time with our pets.
>
> We will treasure and honor their memories. We will think of them constantly. Topper, Triptych, Tripper, Trio,

and Tess were very special and loving animals. Years from now, we will continue to hold them in our hearts and share stories of our adventures together.

We will not be reluctant or ashamed to express the grief we feel for our departed pets. We understand that grieving is an integral part of the recovery process. The greater injustice would be to not recognize our pain.

Finally, we will continue to work on behalf of dogs and cats everywhere. We were so blessed to be with these five unique animals—this is how we will honor their memory. We want other animals to know a similar joy and to be loved.

The second anniversary of the fire came and went. Charlotte, who hates to be cold, braved the winter snow to fly home to Indianapolis for a holiday visit with her family in mid-December. She made it clear before leaving that this was her way of coping with the impending anniversary. I certainly understood. This time around, I chose to be home on December 14, surrounded by our animals. It was a long night, but I managed with lots of hugs from Charlie and holding Emma as tightly as I could. December used to be our favorite month. Now Charlotte and I see it more as an endurance test.

Three more animals came into our lives in 1999. Catalina, a lovely long-haired beige feline, looks like a piece of shag carpeting from the 1970s. Born without eyes, she was left to wander the streets of neighboring Los Osos by an owner who couldn't understand why a blind cat shouldn't be outdoors. Animal rescue people intervened and Catalina suddenly needed a new home. She found one, mostly under our bed. There are nights we fall asleep to the sounds of gentle purring from below.

Paulette Bishop, a good friend of ours, died unexpectedly in September. She was only fifty-six. Paulette loved life. She loved cats even more. Charlotte and I both spoke at her memorial service and agonized over how best to pay tribute to Paulette's memory. We soon found ourselves standing in the cat room at Animal Services, staring at the steel cages brimming with kittens. Most cages had litters of two, three, four meowing kittens, calling out for attention. In the center, however, staring right at us, was a solitary black-and-white kitten sticking her paw playfully through the door. Her card indicated she had been picked up more than a week ago. Time was running out for her. We named her Pauley. She now runs the house, even chasing Earl Grey down the hallway.

Then in December, while Charlotte was away, I received a phone call from Larry at Animal Services. He had a young dog, a small dog. "I've been at the pound for six years and this is the sweetest dog I've ever seen out there," Larry said. "But nobody wants her and I can't let them put this dog down." What was the problem? I found out when I showed up at Larry's house that night—he had agreed to foster the dog just to get her off death row. Brown and black in color, she seemed to be some kind of beagle/shepherd mix, weighing maybe twenty-five pounds. What distinguished her, however, was the line of white hair and bare, rubbery skin running down her spine, clear signs of trauma. She might have been hit by a car, or subjected to some type of fire, but this dog was permanently scarred.

Five days later, I drove out to the airport to meet Charlotte. As we walked across the parking lot towards our car, Charlotte was excited to see the dogs in the back of the CRV, eagerly waiting to welcome her home. I unlocked the hatch door so she could greet the dogs personally.

"Hello, everybody," Charlotte said, leaning into the car. "Look, here's my Charlie...and there's my Tanner...and, oh, here's my Simon." All of which was followed by a short pause and an audible gasp as my wife realized there were now four dogs in the car. "And who's this?" she asked, warmly hugging the small, happy dog without hesitation, the dog eventually named Ginger.

Final count: Nine cats. One kitten. Four dogs. Two humans continuing the journey.

Resources

RECOMMENDED READING:

Adamec, Christine, *When Your Pet Dies,* New York: Berkley
  Publishing Group, 1996

Anderson, Moira, *Coping with Sorrow on the Loss of Your Pet,*
  Los Angeles: Peregrine Press, 1987

Harris, Eleanor, *Pet Loss: A Spiritual Guide,* New York: Llewellyn
  Publications, 1997

Knapp, Caroline, *Pack of Two: The Intricate Bond Between People
  and Dogs,* New York: Dial, 1998

Kowalski, Gary, *Goodbye, Friend; Healing Wisdom to Anyone Who
  Has Ever Lost a Pet,* Walpole, NH: Stillpoint Publishing, 1997

Kowalski, Gary, *The Souls of Animals,* Walpole, NH: Stillpoint
  Publishing, 1991

Lemieux, Christina, *Coping with the Loss of a Pet—A Gentle Guide
  for All Who Love a Pet,* Reading, PA: Wallace R. Clark & Co., 1992

Nieburg, Harry and Fischer, Arlene, *Pet Loss: A Thoughtful Guide
  for Adults and Children,* New York: Harper & Row, 1985

Quackenbush, Jamie and Graveline, Denise, *When Your Pet Dies:
  How to Cope With Your Feelings,* New York: Simon & Schuster, 1985

Sife, Wallace, *The Loss of a Pet,* New York: Howell Book House, 1998

PET GRIEF TELEPHONE HOTLINES: A friendly voice is just a phone call away. Most of these lines are staffed by trained veterinary students across the country.

The Pet Loss Support Group (918) 627-9795

Chicago Veterinary Medical Association (708) 603-3994

Cornell University College of Veterinary Medicine (607) 253-3932

University of Florida College of Veterinary Medicine
(352) 392-4700, ext. 4080

Iowa State University College of Veterinary Medicine Pet Loss
Support Hotline (888) ISU-PLSH

Michigan State University College of Veterinary Medicine
(517) 372-2300

Ohio State University College of Veterinary Medicine
(614) 292-1823

San Diego County Pet Bereavement Program (619) 275-0728

St. Hubert's Animal Welfare Center, Madison, NJ (973) 377-7094

Tufts University (Boston) School of Veterinarian Medicine
(508) 839-7966

University of California at Davis School of Veterinary Medicine
(916) 752-4200

Professional Organizations: The Delta Society, based in Renton, Washington, is a nonprofit humane organization promoting the interaction of people, animals, and the environment. It maintains a variety of helpful materials, including a national directory of pet loss counselors and support groups, videotapes on pet loss, and a 100-page booklet on pet loss and bereavement. (800) 869-6898.

The American Veterinary Medical Association offers support through a special publication, *Pet Loss, Do I Know When It Is Time?* 800-248-AVMA.

The Association for Pet Loss and Bereavement (APLB), based in Brooklyn, New York, is a nonprofit organization whose membership includes counselors and authors in the field of pet grief. APLB offers a regular newsletter and serves as a clearinghouse of pet grief information and supporting materials. P.O. Box 106, Brooklyn, New York, 11230, *www.aplb.org.*

Internet Resources: At *www.lavamind.com,* there is Virtual Pet Cemetery where, for a small donation, you can leave an "epitaph" for your departed animal companion. It is an emotionally powerful experience to read tribute after tribute—you come away knowing that you are not alone in your pain and loss.

The first newsgroup established exclusively for grieving pet owners can be found at *alt.support.grief.pet-loss.*

Rivendell Resources, a private counseling group in Ann Arbor, Michigan, offers on-line support at *rivendell.org/support groups.* Though it deals with all forms of grief, Rivendell recently added options specifically in the area of pet grief.

Other valuable on-line listings of pet loss resources can be found at *www.foreverpets.com* and *www.netwalk.com* a.k.a. "Lightning Strike." Each site provides information on relevant books and other support materials. The Lightning Strike listing, created to "provide lightning fast assistance and support for the grieving owners of dead, dying, sick and missing animals," is especially impressive. This site offers everything from counseling information to sending a pet-loss sympathy card via email.

Hundreds of individual web sites have been created as personal memorials, complete with photos, for departed pets. While not providing specific support information, the heartfelt loss is obvious. You scroll through these and think: *This is exactly how I'm feeling.*

SPECIAL CEREMONIES: Departed pets from around the world are remembered and honored every Monday night in a special candlelight ceremony. You are invited to light a candle in your home at 7 p.m. (PST) in memory of your pets.

Visit *www.petloss.com* to learn more about this universal gathering. Also, the International Association of Pet Cemeteries has designated the second Sunday in September as *National Pet Memorial Day.* The day is intended to remember all beloved companion animals and their lasting contributions to our lives.

About The Authors

THE BOOK: David Congalton lives in San Luis Obispo, California. He is a popular radio/news talk-show host with a daily three-hour show, "The Dave Congalton Show," which debuted in 1992. He also writes a monthly pet column for *Plus* magazine as well as writing for several national magazines on veterinary health care. In addition, Congalton is the executive director of The Cuesta College Writer's Conference.

With a masters degree in communication, Congalton taught college courses in speech and mass media at De Pauw University, Concordia College in Minnesota, and the University of Tulsa, among others. After migrating to California, Congalton was a columnist for the *San Luis Obispo County Telegram-Tribune* for eight years. Presently, Congalton uses his talking and writing skills as a humane educator on behalf of animals. *Three Cats, Two Dogs* is Congalton's first book.

THE FOREWORD: Wallace Sife, Ph.D., wrote the foreword to *Three Cats, Two Dogs*. He is a pioneer in the field of pet bereavement as well as a noted psychologist, author, and lecturer on pet loss. He is also the founder and president of the Association for Pet Loss and Bereavement (APLB). Dr. Sife is the author of *The Loss of a Pet* (Howell Book House 1998).

Other Titles by NewSage Press

NewSage Press has published several titles related to animals, in particular books that respect all animals and their essential presence in the web of life. We hope our books on animals as our companions and fellow inhabitants of earth will move humanity towards more compassionate and respectful treatment of all living beings. Among those titles are:

Singing to the Sound: Visions of Nature, Animals, and Spirit
by Brenda Peterson

Blessing the Bridge: What Animals Teach Us About Death, Dying, and Beyond
by Rita M. Reynolds (Available August 2000)

Dancer on the Grass: True Stories About Horses and People
by Teresa Tsimmu Martino

Unforgettable Mutts: Pure of Heart Not of Breed
by Karen Derrico

Conversations with Animals: Cherished Messages and Memories as Told by an Animal Communicator
by Lydia Hiby with Bonnie Weintraub

Food Pets Die For: Shocking Facts About Pet Food
by Ann N. Martin

The Wolf, the Woman, the Wilderness; A True Story of Returning Home
by Teresa Tsimmu Martino

NewSage Press

For more information about other NewSage Press titles, visit our web site at

www.newsagepress.com

or request a catalog directly from NewSage Press.

PO Box 607
Troutdale, OR 97060-0607

Phone Toll Free (877) 695-2211
Fax (503) 695-5406
Email newsage@teleport.com